ABOUT THIS SERIES

....But after that, I realised that I knew very little about these parents of mine. They had been born about the start of the Twentieth Century, and they died in 1970 and 1980. For their last 20 years, I was old enough to speak with a bit of sense.

I could have talked to them a lot about their lives. I could have found out about the times they lived in. But I did not. I know almost nothing about them really. Their courtship? Working in the pits? The Lock-out in the Depression? Losing their second child? Being dusted as a miner? The shootings at Rothbury? My uncles killed in the War? Love on the dole? There were hundreds, thousands of questions that I would now like to ask them. But, alas, I can't. It's too late.

Thus, prompted by my guilt, I resolved to write these books. They describe happenings that affected people, real people. The whole series is, to coin a modern phrase, designed to push your buttons, to make you remember and wonder at things forgotten.

The books might just let nostalgia see the light of day, so that oldies and youngies will talk about the past and re-discover a heritage otherwise forgotten. Hopefully, they will spark discussions between generations, and foster the asking and answering of questions that should not remain unanswered.

BORN IN 1953?

WHAT ELSE HAPPENED?

RON WILLIAMS

AUSTRALIAN SOCIAL HISTORY

BOOK 15 IN A SERIES OF 35
FROM 1939 to 1973

War Babies Years (1939 to 1945):   7 Titles
Baby Boom Years (1946 to 1960): 15 Titles
Post Boom Years (1961 to 1970):   13 Titles

BOOM, BOOM BABY, BOOM

BORN IN 1953? WHAT ELSE HAPPENED?
Published by Boom Books.
Wickham, NSW, Australia
Web: www.boombooks.biz
Email: jen@boombooks.biz

© Ron Williams 2012.   This edition 2023.

Creator: Williams, Ron, 1934- author
Title: Born in 1953? : what else happened? / Ron Williams.
Edition: ISBN: 9780994601537 (paperback)
Australia--History--Miscellanea--20th century.

Cover   images: Alexander   Turnbull   Library,
Wellington,   NewZealand, 1/2-020196-F, Edmund Hillary (by
John Pascoe);
National Archives of Australia.
A1805, CU43/17, Hoad and Rosewall win Davis Cup;
A1200, L15690, family breakfast;
A1200, L17264, piano singalong.

TABLE OF CONTENTS

IMPORTANT PEOPLE AND RESULTS

Queen of England	Elizabeth II
Prime Minister of Oz	Robert Menzies
Leader of Opposition	Doc Evatt
The Pope	Pius XII
US President	D Eisenhower
PM of Britain	Winston Churchill

Governor General:

Till May 8th	William McKell
After May 8th	Sir Williams Slim

HOLDER OF ASHES:

1950 - 1951	Australia	4 - 0
1953	England	1 - 0
1954 - 1955	England	3 - 1

MELBOURNE CUP WINNERS:

1952	Dalray
1953	Wodalla
1954	Rising Fast

ACADEMY AWARDS:

Best Actor	William Holden
Best Actress	Audrey Hepburn
Best Movie	Here to Eternity

PREFACE TO THIS SERIES: 1939 TO 1973

This book is the fifteenth in a series of books that I aim to publish. It tells a story about a number of important or newsworthy events that happened in 1953. The series will cover each of the years from 1939 to 1973, for a total of 35 books, which should just about bring me to the end of my thoroughly undistinguished writing career.

I developed my interest in writing these books a few years ago at a time when my children entered their teens. My own teens started in 1947, and I started trying to remember what had happened to me then. I thought of the big events first, like Saturday afternoon at the pictures, and cricket in the back yard, and the wonderful fun of going to Maitland on the train for school each day. Then I recalled some of the not-so-good things. I was an altar boy, and that meant three or four Masses a week. I might have thought I loved God at that stage, but I really hated his Masses. And the schoolboy bullies, like Greg Favell, and the hapless Freddie Bevan. Yet, to compensate for these, there was always the beautiful, black-headed, blue-sailor-suited June Brown, who I was allowed to worship from a distance.

I also thought about my parents. Most of the major events that I lived through came to mind readily. But after that, I realised that I really knew very little about these parents of mine. They had been born about the start of the Twentieth Century, and they died in 1970 and 1980. For their last 20 years, I was old enough to speak with a bit of sense. I could have talked to them a lot about their lives. I could have found out about the times they lived in. But I did not. I know almost nothing about them really. Their courtship?

Working in the pits? The Lock-out in the Depression? Losing their second child? Being dusted as a miner? The shootings at Rothbury? My uncles killed in the War? There were hundreds, thousands of questions that I would now like to ask them. But, alas, I can't. It's too late.

Thus, prompted by my guilt, I resolved to write these books. They describe happenings that affected people, real people. In 1953, there is some coverage of international affairs, but a lot more on social events within Australia. This book, and the whole series is, to coin a modern phrase, designed to push the reader's buttons, to make you remember and wonder at things forgotten. The books might just let nostalgia see the light of day, so that oldies and youngies will talk about the past and re-discover a heritage otherwise forgotten. Hopefully, they will spark discussions between generations, and foster the asking and the answering of questions that should not remain unanswered.

The sources of my material. I was born in 1934, so that I can remember well a great deal of what went on around me from 1946 onwards. But of course, the bulk of this book's material came from research. That meant that I spent many hours in front of a computer reading electronic versions of newspapers, magazines, Hansard, Ministers' Press releases and the like. My task was to sift out, **day-by-day**, those stories and events that would be of interest to the most readers. Then I supplemented these with materials from books, broadcasts, memoirs, biographies, government reports and statistics. And I talked to old-timers, one-on-one, and in organised groups, and to Baby Boomers about their recollections. People with stories to tell come out of the woodwork, and talk no end about the tragic and funny and commonplace events that have shaped their lives.

The presentation of each book. For each year covered, the end result is a collection of short Chapters on many of the topics that concerned ordinary people in that year. I think I have covered most of the major issues that people then were interested in. On the other hand, in some cases I have dwelt a little on minor frivolous matters, perhaps to the detriment of more sober considerations. Still, in the long run, this makes the book more readable, and hopefully it will convey adequately the spirit of the times.

Each of the books is mainly Sydney based, but I have been **deliberately national in outlook**, so that readers elsewhere will feel comfortable that I am talking about matters that affected them personally. After all, housing shortages and strikes and a tuberculosis epidemic involved all Australians, and other issues, such as problems overseas, had no State component in them. Overall, I expect I can **make you wonder, remember, rage and giggle equally**, no matter where you hail from.

THOUGHTS FROM 1952

The world had seen a lot of tough times since the start of WWII in 1939. Firstly, there were the dreadful seven years of the Wars in Europe and the Asia-Pacific. This was a period marred by thoughts and reality of death, of long-term separation from loved ones, of austerity and rationing, and of **repression of freedoms for the common good**.

This was followed by a period of five years, from mid-1945, for half a decade, when Australians slowly kicked the War habit. There was diminishing need for austerity, rationing could be relaxed, regulations and constraints could be lifted. The world was a better place, a safer place, but still there was the shadow of the dreadful War years haunting many lives. As well, there were the many killjoys in high positions who had enjoyed the power that War had given them, and who stood firmly in the way of returning to normal. Thus, for example, butter rationing continued till 1949, and petrol rationing till 1950. Price controls on rents, and on most goods and services, on banking, on imports, on what-have-you, were still very evident. Still, there were fewer blackouts and no tank traps on the beaches, and it was all much, much better than War. Though, as a young lad, I did miss the searchlights at night.

The fun started about 1950, and continued then for years. After Bob Menzies got his title of Prime Minister back, the Baby Boomers took over. In 1952, this horde of revellers were now having their second child, starting to build a house in the developing housing estates on the fringes of cities, and buying a car on hire purchase. Hills Hoist sales were booming, jobs were easy to get in most years, electric lawn-mowers could be afforded, and everyone by now had a 40-hour week. So life was good and getting better.

By 1953, however, there were several events that marred the situation. The Korean War had started in 1950 and was still dragging on. This war was supposedly a Civil War between North and South Korea, but was really just a trial of strength between the Capitalist US, on the one hand, and Communist China and Russia, on the other. The battle-lines had moved south, then moved north, up to the border with China. About that time, the US Commander, Douglas MacArthur was keen to press on and take on the full might of the Chinese and Russian States. But that would have involved another world War. So, when he persisted, **he was sacked by President Truman, and sent home to America.** Meanwhile the fighting continued, and the battle-lines now settled around the 38th Parallel, near the middle of the Korean peninsula. Negotiations between the interested parties, and with the UN, were always going on, but no one was at all serious about these, and there was no hope that peace might break out soon.

Politically, Prime Minster Bob Menzies was still trying to scare the nation with his never-ending campaign against Communism, and had tried to outlaw that Party. In 1951 he held a national referendum on the matter, but it failed. At the same time, all young men of 18 years of age were now being conscripted into National Service, for 14 weeks in the first year, and for follow-up periods over the next three years. This was all part of **the Red menace theme that Menzies continued to push**.

The most immediate problem for most people was that, right from the start of 1952, the national economy had started to go downhill. Then the Treasurer, Arthur Fadden, had introduced measures on a large scale that tried to stop the nation from spending so much, and actually cut off access to many goods that he deemed luxuries. The measures were extremely unpopular. As the year progressed, inflation appeared to boom, up to an annual rate of 20 per cent, and for a few months everyone was really worried. Then in October, the quarterly figure for inflation came in at 6 per cent, and so, with a sigh of relief, things got back to normal.

In December 1952, Fadden make an important speech, in the Christmas spirit, in which he said that things were on the improve, and that next year the nation would become its old, prosperous self. Good times were just around the corner. **Only the very gullible took any notice of him.** Granted, the wheat crop had been a bumper one, and the price of wool was slightly on the increase. But our balances of Sterling currency were still too low, import restrictions curtailed much business activity, unemployment was worrying and growing, and those luxuries were nowhere to be seen. Still, maybe Fadden knew something that others did not, so we will keep an eye on his forecasts as we proceed.

One great feature of Oz life in 1952 was the rapid formation of families, and the increase in the tempo of life as a result. Most people by now had thrown off the melancholy of the post-War years, and were wanting to get on with the business of living. The returned Servicemen were nowhere near as restrained as their 1930's-weary parents were, and were ready to make the world a better place. They wanted nice new houses, lawn mowers, Hills Hoists, interesting jobs, and motor cars. They liked their new barbies on Sunday afternoons, some liked a punt on the horses on Saturdays, others saw a movie in a theatre every week, and Saturday night dances at the local hall were often on the agenda. The women wanted their cosmetics and magazines and new Labor-saving household appliances, and were out to reduce the household drudgery that their mothers knew so well.

So, when 1953 dawned under a bit of an economic cloud, they were not daunted into cutting back their aspirations and spending, but instead looked for the turn-round that they **knew** was certain to come soon.

There was one big blot on this scene, right round the nation. This was the availability and price of housing. I won't spend much time on it here, because we will hear a lot about it as the year progresses. Let me just say that the supply of houses had not increased much since the start of the War. One cause of this was that in 1940 the various governments decided to fix rents at the then current levels.

Believe it or not, they were still fixed at those same 1940 levels. So that no landlord in the nation would build a single house for renting.

Add to that, new families were being formed at a boom rate, and about 100,000 migrants were flooding into the country each year. Put it all together, and there was a major problem developing.

Having said that, we are ready for the bright New Year. Except for one page of material below, that explains the rules I set in writing this series of books.

MY RULES IN WRITING THESE BOOKS

NOTE. Throughout this book, I rely a lot on reproducing **Letters** from the newspapers. Whenever I do this, I put the text in a different font, and indent it a little, and make the font somewhat smaller. **I do not edit the text at all**. That is, I do not correct spelling or grammar. If the text gets at all garbled, I do not correct it. It's just as it was seen in the Papers.

SECOND NOTE. The material for each book, when it comes from newspapers, is reported as it was seen at the time. **If** the benefit of hindsight over the years changes things, then I **might** record that in my **Comments**. The information reported thus reflects matters **as they were seen in 1953.**

THIRD NOTE. Let me also apologise in advance to anyone I might offend. In a work such as this, it is certain some people will think I got some things wrong. I am sure that I did, but please remember, all of this is **only my opinion.** And really, **my opinion does not matter one little bit in the scheme of things. I hope you will say "silly old bugger", shrug your shoulders, and read on.**

FOURTH NOTE. Let me remind you that the writers of Letters to the newspapers did so with pen and ink. In the early years, this was really laborious, with **a pen and nib, and ink-well, and a blotte**r. Over the next thirty years, fountain pens became popular and then some early ball-points came on the scene. Whenever they wrote, it was quite a task, and the fact that **they wrote so many Letters testifies to their passion.**

Having said that, we are ready to go. Hold on to your precious hats.

JANUARY: TV IS COMING?

TV for better or for worse. Australia was a bit of a laggard with regard to the introduction of TV to the nation. Britain had been making public broadcasts since just before for War. So too had America. However, the systems that these two countries used were very different. In Britain, broadcasts were all from Government controlled stations, just as their radio was, through the BBC. In the US, the system was all commercial, with no government stations at all.

One of the questions for Australia was should we favour one of these two possibilities, or should we have a hybrid, some government and some commercial stations. The matter had been settled, so they thought, in 1948 by the Labor Government of Ben Chifley, which opted for the British system in full, and passed legislation to that effect. But the new Menzies Government, by 1953, was flirting with the idea of a hybrid solution.

Other factors were under discussion. What should be the hours of broadcasting? In Britain, they had been restricted to a few hours in the morning, then a few hours in the afternoon, then four hours at night. America mainly just started in the mornings and finished late at night.

Then there were comparisons of the quality of the two existing systems. Britain was reported, by some, to have some very good shows, of high intellectual standard, and moral and conservative. But others said that they were stuffy and boring. The standard of American shows was generally agreed to be a lot lower, with few high quality shows. But that led to the question of what we wanted from TV? Did we want it to be educational and supporting strict moral codes, or did we want it to reflect the general population with its looser standards, and love of frivolity?

The questions grew and grew. You can imagine what the Churches said, and you can equally well imagine what the various commercial interests wanted. In late December, 1952, various people went public with very robust arguments both for and against lots of suggestions, but the Christmas break seemed to have quelled the raging fires. So that, in the first two weeks of January, only these three moderate Letters below were printed in the *Sydney Morning Herald* (*SMH*).

Letters, J Ernest Benson.   The recent controversy on the question of television emphasises the age-long attitude of the human mind to technological progress.

We should take heed lest, once again, in our almost superstitious mistrust of the unknown, we fail to see in this new medium a clear example of that "tide in the affairs of men which, taken at the flood, leads on to fortune." Or maybe misfortune?

Television is not merely a medium of mass entertainment; it is essentially a means of extending human vision almost without limit with vast potentialities in educational, scientific and industrial applications. When combined with sound transmission in the form of television broadcasting, it provides the most powerful means of human communication yet established.

Television's use in that sphere, for the achievement of better understanding between groups in society and between Governments and people and, therefore, as a means of stimulating cooperative effort for the development of our country, is limited only by human ingenuity and imagination.

Letters, R Everson. A suggestion has been made by Pastor R A Anderson that television is a potentially great religious medium. Wherever else the greatness of TV may lie, the facts indicate that any greatness in this field is certainly latent, if it is there at all.

Mr Wayne Coy, addressing the US National Association of Radio and Television Broadcasters last year, pointed out that religion received on the average 0.9 per cent of TV transmitting time in USA – that is, nearly four and a half minutes per eight-hour day.

Letters, A Dedman. J Ernest Benson calls television "the most powerful means of human communication yet established." This emphasises its potential dangers in harmful or unqualified hands.

There is a fear that such means of communication could mould the mass mind too readily. And what shall it profit us, as a nation, to gain the expensive contrivance of television, and lose our capacity for critical reasoning?

Then, in mid-January, **the Government removed one uncertainty**. It committed itself to **a hybrid system, with no humming or hawing**. The next day, it announced that a Royal Commission would be set up to examine all aspects of the introduction of TV. It was acknowledged that this might delay the start-up by about six months, but the idea was that the need for urgency was not so great.

The *SMH* Editorial thought this was a good move. It had earlier warned against a solely Government system because it would make possible the rise of a monopoly that might one day be used against the interests of the people. It also said the Royal Commission gave everyone, including the Churches and promoters, an opportunity to present their views in a sober forum, with enough room for rebuttal and counter argument.

ABORIGINES

The Church of England's Dean, Doctor Barton Babbage, was about to leave Sydney's St Andrews Cathedral to take up a position as Principal at the Ridley Theological College in Melbourne. In leaving, perhaps he felt that he could speak his mind strongly on a matter that concerned him. In any case, he came out, at the end of January, with both barrels blazing on the subject of Aborigines.

In his final sermon, he said that "our native policy is indefensible in theory, and disastrous in practice. On the one hand, it does not protect the Aborigines on reserves from the depredations of whites. On the other hand, it neither facilitates their advance towards civilisation nor their ultimate assimilation. Our many words of sympathy are mocked by the thousands of degraded and depressed people who crouch on the edge of rubbish heaps throughout the continent.

"Our first duty as Christians is one of penance and shame. We have sinned against the Aborigines, both decimating and destroying them. Our second duty, as Christians, is one of reparation and restitution. The fact remains that we have not yet begun to make adequate amends.

"We have a responsibility for the welfare of the Aborigines **whatever the views of the graziers and planters to the north**. It is a national scandal and disgrace that the original inhabitants of this continent should still be deprived of the most elementary democratic rights. Nothing will be gained by our current policy of **segregation**. We cannot gain, even if we banish the Aborigines to barren reserves or restrict them to squalid ghettoes. Our goal must be that of eventual **assimilation of the whole Aboriginal population.**"

Such views could not be left unchallenged. In particular, Mr Michael Sawtell did a great hatchet job, as you will see below. Mr Sawtell was a member of the NSW Aborigines Wefare Board until 1962. For 20-odd of the years that I cover in the writing of this Series, Sawtell was persistent in expesssing his views through the columns of the *SMH*. His opinions, on Aborigines and outback issues, were always clearly expressed and worthy of consideration, whether you agreed with him or not. Here, he is at his outspoken best.

Letters, Michael Sawtell. I am astounded that the Dean of Sydney, Dr S Barton Babbage, should make such misleading statements about the present conditions of our Aborigines.

Evidently the Dean does not know that everything possible is now being done all over Australia to help our Aborigines to become good citizens. **In the past** our treatment of the Aborigines may not have been so enlightened, but **that it is all finished now**, so why harp on the past?

It is impossible to keep Aborigines on their reserves, for when they hear about the delights of the white man's towns, they must go and have a look for themselves. When the squatters build huts for the Aborigines, who are never keen on houses, the Aborigines store their belongings in the hut and sleep outside, and if there is a death, they burn the hut down.

All over Australia Aborigines are members of trade-unions and receive the same pay as white men, except in some instances where the pay is held in trust for them.

Since the War, the Aborigines' Welfare Board of NSW has spent 500,000 Pounds on houses for Aborigines that many white people would be pleased to live in. Now we cannot get back a penny of rent from Aborigines earning up to 20 Pounds a week as shearers. The Board will also put any Aboriginal through the university, if we can find one who can pass the qualifying examination.

It is impossible to detribalise and to Christianise our Aborigines without demoralising them. **The greatest factor in the demoralisation of our Aborigines is Christianity.** The Churches **destroy the Aborigines' faith in their own religion**, and when you destroy a man's faith, you destroy his soul.

The Churches do much good for the Aborigines, but they also do much harm. Civilisation offers great opportunities to native races, for both good and ill.

The Editor of the *SMH*, and the distinguished scholar, Professor A Elkin, and also the Federal Minister for Native Affairs, all responded with arguments that, between them, said that Babbage was 20 years out of date. Also, the policy of segregation to reserves was possibly a failure, or at least under serious consideration. They added that the single concept of "Aborigines" was a delusion. That in fact, native Australians ranged from the most primitive persons living in squalor in the deep outback, right through to the most sophisticated living in our major cities with considerable wealth. Professor Elkin added that the policy of segregation had to give way to assimilation, and for that to succeed, all Australians needed to accept the fact that Aborigines were acceptable at the individual and social level in all spheres. **Dean Babbage re-entered the fray.**

Letters, S Barton Babbage. Mr Sawtell is astounded by my comments on Australian native policy. I am equally astounded that Mr Sawtell should have used this occasion to make an unwarranted and **unjust attack on the missionary work of the church**.

I quoted the comments of the Minister for Native Affairs (Mr Paul Hasluck) in support of my contention that our native ministration gives ground for concern. Mr Hasluck said: "Our record of native administration will not stand scrutiny at the standard of our professions, publicly made in the forum of the world, of a high concern for human welfare. We should be condemned out of our own mouths if those professions were measured by the standard of native administration accepted in Australia today.

This is the statement of a responsible Minister of the Crown. Further, it does not describe, as Professor Elkin suggests, a state of affairs which existed 20 years ago: on the contrary, it describes conditions which existed, to be exact, on June 8, 1950.

The gravamen of my charge was that the Aborigines are herded into steadily diminishing reserves, and that their progress towards assimilation is being unduly retarded because of inadequate educational facilities and social amenities.

As an illustration, I may mention the recent violation of the Great Central Aboriginal Reserve, guaranteed by the Federal Government, for **the construction of the rocket range**. These are the things which blacken the good name of Australia in the councils of the world.

Comment. All the above opinions came from people walking the halls of power. There were also Letters from many unknowns who spoke of the segregation versus assimilation debate in more practical terms, in what they actually experienced. This letter below is typical.

Letters, J J Wallington. Mr Sawtell and Professor Elkin say the policy on Aborigines is on the right track. Then it is time somebody set the policy in motion, because, as an observer in this district, I can't see anything being done for them.

It is definitely as Dean Babbage says. They live in tin shanties here and at Gular, Walgett, and Pilliga, in very primitive conditions. Mr Sawtell says his board spent 500,000 Pounds on housing for them. I guess they would like to know where and how many houses, for there is no accommodation in this town for the unfortunates.

Comment. Mr Wallington has a point. That figure of 500,000 Pounds would not have built many houses. It sounds a lot, but hardly scratched the surface.

Second Comment. What to do with racial minorities had exercised minds for quite a while. Remember that the US had earlier sent the Indians to reserves in their outback, and had plied them with financial assistance in an effort to build independent self-supporting communities. This was part of the Australian idea behind settling our natives in reserves.

Remember that the world had just seen a huge evacuation of Muslims in India to Pakistan, and the reverse migration of Hindus from that country back to India. The idea of segregation in "reserves" was a familiar one.

Assimilation did in fact, over the next two decades, become the dominant approach. No one can be certain even now, around 2020. that it is as good as was hoped. For example, how well have we assimilated new migrants from the Middle East and Central Europe? It seems that now the idea is on the nose in some quarters, though what the alternative is seems to lack coherent support.

PETS IN CHURCH

Letters, Jean Campbell. It was gratifying to read of the service last Sunday in St Mark's Church, Granville, to which children brought animals to be blessed. For many years these beautiful and touching services have been held in numbers of churches in England, and the rector of St Mark's has set a fine example, which, if followed by other members of the clergy, should incline the young minds of our future citizens towards an aspect of love, service, and responsibility which is often neglected in this country.

Letters, C Weston. Jean Campbell is welcome to her opinion on the practice of having Church services for pet animals, but I think it is childish and impious and certainly has no scriptural authority.

The last thing the church should indulge in in these momentous times – times which demand a clear-cut and virile testimony and witness – is a sentimental practice such as this. The fact that various churches in Britain and/or elsewhere have adopted this practice is no evidence of its value and rightness. Rather is it, in my opinion, an indication how far some ministers of religion have deviated from the commission of their Divine Master, and how clouded their spiritual perspective and vision has become.

Letters, H Baker. C Weston has been misled by a worthy intensity of conviction into making far too much of the recent church services at Granville. It turned out that I was the only clergyman in the congregation, and I can therefore remove some mistaken impressions.

The service was as reverent as anybody could desire. The interpretation suggested to my mind was that it expressed the divinely planned association of men and animals, which was shared by our Lord. It conveyed some sense of the wholeness and unity of life. It might appeal specially to children, but was certainly appreciated by adults. In any case, to achieve such an expression is not at all "childish," but very difficult.

The pets were scarcely visible. The beloved canine friends of two small boys had thoughts of a sporting engagement, but were efficiently advised by their masters in a matter of seconds. A clutch of chickens sang when the congregation sang, and was removed to the porch – in my opinion, unnecessarily. A little girl moved diffidently in the aisle to see "who" was in church. There is nothing impious about all that. It was very charming, and our Lord could be charming, as well as severe.

Letters, (Rev) J Johnstone. Would Mr Baker regard with the same approval a move by boys at The King's School, where he is chaplain, to bring pets to his chapel services or his Divinity lessons in school hours?

In any case, where is the line to be drawn? Some enterprising citizen of Parramatta or Rosehill might feel that his pet racehorse would benefit from the experience.

FEBRUARY: POST SCRIPT ON SAWTELL

In the previous chapter, Michael Sawtell spoke up about certain facets of Aboriginal life. In particular, he argued that assimilation was not a good policy, and that the Christian Churches were destroying Aboriginal culture.

In February, he spoke up again along the same lines, and got a second batch of protests. This is not surprising, given that he was uttering real fighting words. His views were well ahead of the rest of the population, which only now was coming to think that assimilation was the right way to go. To go way beyond this and say that assimilation was a damaging influence, and that tribal culture should be the basis for native advancement, was too far, too fast. So the support he got for his views, as published by the *SMH*, was nil. No Letters of support were published.

Letters that disagreed with him, however, were more plentiful. I enclose three such.

Letters, M Warren, Secretary, Australian Board of Missions. It is not easy to follow the argument of Mr Sawtell. In the facts that the tribal life of the Aborigines is being broken up, and that their future lies in assimilation by the white race, the Church sees its clear duty to come to their assistance, and to fit them by education and the Christian religion for the new conditions.

To quote Mr Sawtell: "It is impossible to keep Aborigines on their reserves"; "All over Australia Aborigines are members of trade-unions and receive the same pay as white men"; "The Aborigines' Welfare Board of NSW will put any Aboriginal through the university..."; "It is impossible to detribalise the Aborigines without demoralising them." But it is surely the first we have heard of the extraordinary charge that to Christianise them also results in their demoralisation.

Are we to understand that Christianity can bring the highest good to every race except the Aboriginal? Or is it that the Christian religion is inferior to that of the Aboriginal and less adequate as a way of life even under the changed conditions?

One wonders how the Aboriginal would retain and practise his primitive tribal religion inside our own industrial set-up.

Australian Governments – and many outside Australia – have watched closely the work of Christian missions over the years and have had ample opportunity to assess its value. Their action in calling the Church more and more to their assistance indicates the conclusion they have reached.

Letters, R Clive Teece. Mr Michael Sawtell writes "The greatest factor in the demoralisation of our Aborigines is Christianity. The Churches destroy the Aborigines' faith in their own religion, and when you destroy a man's faith you destroy his soul."

I would point out that the Anglo-Saxons, Scots, Picts, Celts, and Britons, who were the races who constituted the early population of Great Britain and Ireland, were originally heathen tribes and were converted at various times to Christianity.

The Christian missions, which effected that conversion, all destroyed the faith of those races in their own religion. They certainly did not destroy their souls. Anyone with any knowledge of history knows that the influence of the Christian religion on the civilisation of the English, Scots, and Irish is inestimable.

Letters, (Pastor) A E Wattsgh. It is to be fervently hoped that other members of the Aborigines' Welfare Board of NSW do not share the view of Mr Michael

Sawtell that "The greatest factor in the demoralisation of our Aborigines is Christianity."

To see the value of Christianity in the development of native populations, one has only to compare natives who have been reared round the wharves of, say, Suva, with those who have been trained on mission stations. Christianity does not destroy a man's faith as Mr Sawtell affirms – it builds a stronger and durable faith on sound premises.

"The greatest factor in the demoralisation of our Aborigines" is that while native races believe Christianity is the white man's religion, they meet so many whites who are not motivated by Christian principles and in many instances have a lower moral standard than the natives themselves.

Comment One. Sawtell's claim had wide consequences if it was universally applied. For example, for hundreds of years, Christians had gone off to the non-European countries and had settled with the natives, black, brown and white, and tried to get converts. These brave souls were so convinced that their religion, this Christianity, was the only right one that they deliberately went forth and propagated it, mostly heedless that they were destroying the culture and the beliefs in the host nations.

Comment two. In defence of Sawtell, let me say that he was a man with 20 years of actual face-to-face experience of Aborigines in their camps and every sort of environment. All the other three respondents appear to have little or none of this first-hand experience. Without wishing to take sides here, I would be more likely to be impressed by the man who was often on the spot than many men who have rarely had that experience.

THREE ARGUMENTS ABOUT WOOL

Eighteen months ago, when the Korean War was being fought as if it mattered, the Korean winter was freezing ground-troops to death, and armies on both sides needed uniforms that kept their soldiers warm until they were killed. Wool was thought to be the perfect fabric to do this, so the demand for it sky-rocketed for about two years. By now, demand had returned to normal, and the price was falling and the volume traded was also down. Australia was a major seller of wool, and in fact it was our major export so, all in all, the wool trade and the nation were close to the doldrums.

Events over the last few years were making the situation worse, and debate on this centred on three arguments. In **the first argument**, research in Britain and America was producing a number of new fibres, such as nylon and orlon that, while they did not have all the wonderful characteristics of wool, were able to compete on a number of different levels. For example, the new fabrics would dry much faster, would in some cases not need ironing, and generally were cheaper.

Letters, M Lipson, Wool Textile Research Laboratory, Geelong. There are several major characteristics of wool which make it outstanding as a textile fibre. One of the most important is its high moisture absorption. Wool has the capacity to absorb up to 30 per cent of water without becoming wet. Garments made from wool can be worn next to the skin and will absorb perspiration without feeling cold and clammy. Synthetics do not possess this desirable attribute.

Wool has good dyeing properties and can be easily processed to a variety of fast shades. In contrast there has been much difficulty in dyeing fibres like Orlon and Dacron, and special equipment is needed to obtain satisfactory colours.

Wool fibre is the only major textile raw material which has scales on its surface; these scales allow the fibres to move in one direction only when washed or milled together. This is the basis of the milling process used to obtain special finishes which are possible only with fabrics woven from wool. Examples of such fabrics are those used for heavy overcoats and billiards cloth. It is also the fundamental operation in the felt industry.

An outstanding property of wool fabric is its great ability to recover from compression and to resume its original form. Thus garments made from wool tend to maintain their shape during wear. Professor Hunter has mentioned that a Dacron suit can be hosed down with water yet retain its shape. But if you wear a Dacron suit and are caught in a heavy shower, then you will be wet through, even though the suit maintains its creases.

Dacron fabrics tend to "pill" on wearing, that is they form small balls of fibres on the surface of the fabric. They are also liable to develop holes or stains due to cigarette and pipe ash because of Dacron's low melting point. Orlon fabrics, although displaying great resistance to outdoor exposure, will be limited in their use because they readily burn. Another disadvantage of the synthetics is that they easily become soiled during wear.

The increase in world demand has been sufficient to utilise all fibres that can be produced, and the continued increase in world population at the rate of 20 million a year, together with rising living standards, should still absorb all available textile raw materials.

Scientific research, as emphasised by Professor Hunter, will be an important factor in deciding the ultimate picture.

Given price stability and efficient application of research results, there should be no cause for despair over the future of wool.

Comment. The argument about what to do about synthetics lasted for decades. Over the **next few years**, a levy was introduced on all woolgrowers that allowed money for research and promotion. As time went on, support for this levy waxed and waned, and arguments about who should pay it, and at what level of payments, were non-stop. Nevertheless, it seems, 60 years later, that this approach has done its bit to keep wool competitive with other materials, along with the host of mixes of wool and synthetics that have developed over the years.

The second argument about our wool markets dwelt on whether wool **alone** would continue to provide livings for graziers. Perhaps they needed to switch half their resources to growing lamb and mutton meat for export. The Letter below sums up some of the issues.

Letters, D A S Campbell. It was pointed out that during the last 10 years there has been an absolute and relative decline in the production of merino wool in Australia, and that this has been largely due to the practice of converting, by official action, merino sheep country into areas suitable for the production of dual-purpose sheep, which means the increasing of sheep numbers used to **produce food**.

As merino wool has been, is still, and is likely to be for a long time, the principal pillar of our export trade, it does not seem to be overestimating the position to say that any policy which reduces the strength of this pillar is an "economic extravagance."

Mr Date is quite illogical when he suggests that I am not in favour of food production because I am concerned to maintain and improve merino wool production. There is ample scope for both these economic activities in Australia and this is recognised at least, in theory, in official circles. It is the gap between theory and practice which is the present danger, for, whatever the agricultural economist may say, merino wool production is being reduced in many areas for food production purposes. The numbers of merino sheep do not need to be reduced. Just increase the numbers overall. It's not one or the other. It's both of them.

The third argument was concerned with the export of merino rams. These superb creatures produced sheep that had the best of wools, in good quantity and, after years of breeding, were virtually unique to Australia. The question became **whether we should export these to other countries** that would use them to enhance their own sheep and would then become competitors against our own wool sales. **Exports of merinos had been banned since 1929.**

In reading the Letter below, I do not suggest you try too hard to follow the arguments. Rather, you might look for evidence of the divided state of the industry, with the great diversity between States, and the great diversity within States, and the difference between producers of rams and the other sheepmen who bought them. It is an unholy mess.

Letters, F Fleming. Your correspondent, Mr Hunt, has made out a superficial case for the retention of the export ban on merino sheep.

However, when he says – "in every year since 1930 with the single exception of 1941, the annual conference of the Graziers' Association of NSW has emphatically rejected the idea of throwing over the ban" – he allows his enthusiasm to exceed the actual facts of the case.

Far from being emphatic in some years, the voting has been very close, and over those years the Graziers' Federal Council and Australian Wool Council, which include representatives from New South Wales, Queensland, Victoria, South Australia, Western Australia, Tasmania, West Darling and Northern Territory, have been fairly consistent in asking for the lifting of the ban.

Mr Hunt belittles the Victorian Graziers' Association because only 36 per cent of Victoria's sheep are merinos (incidentally they produce some of the best fine wool in Australia), while New South Wales sheep are four-fifths merinos. He omits to mention that Queensland, which has a still greater proportion of merinos, has nearly always voted for the lifting of the embargo.

I was, for many years, a member of the executive committee of the NSW Graziers' Association, and attended Graziers' Federal Council and Australian Wool Council meetings. I cannot remember South Australia, another large merino state, ever varying in its opposition to the ban, while many Tasmanians blame it for a number of their studs going out of existence and others reducing their numbers considerably.

Comment. The wool industry was really big business for Australia. After two years of great recent success, harsh reality was making its presence felt, and clearly a new day was dawning. As usual, in a democracy, the reaction of the industry was for many voices and opinions to be heard all at once. Gradually, after many years, numbering decades, it got its act together a lot, but even now (in 2016) no one could say all its various issues have been settled.

BROKEN HILL AND THE LAW

Broken Hill had a reputation around Australia as the equivalent of America's Wild West. It was legendary that hotel hours were scarcely heeded, that gambling was always available, and that women of low repute were affordable.

In recent months, a number of bad reports about the goings-on in Broken Hill had been given much space in the Press, and this was putting pressure on a reluctant Police Force to crack down. Then, the City really got back in the news when the Sydney Press reported that a **trainload of revellers** was coming to Broken Hill soon for the sole purpose of **"enjoying its vice."**

The first letter below expresses the approach that the police had towards the so-called vice there.

Letters, T Kinkead, Ex-Police Inspector. It has been the practice for many years for the police to exercise discretion in dealing with persons of good character where it is considered that a caution will meet the case. This dispenses with arrest and prosecution.

Strictly speaking, this practice may not be in accord with a constable's oath of office. However it is commonsense, and saved thousands of reputable citizens from arrest and conviction. A certain amount of discretionary power must surely be left to members of the Force. Providing it is exercised honestly and with commonsense, it is of immense value.

The attempt to make political capital out of the prevailing conditions at Broken Hill is unfair to the Premier, Mr Cahill, and the Commissioner, Mr Delaney, and to the residents of that city, who have a record as citizens at least equal to any city centre of equal numbers.

In administering the liquor laws and those relating to gambling and betting, due regard has been taken of the isolation of Broken Hill, the absence of ordinary amenities, the severe summer climate, the fact that most residents are shift workers covering the 24 hours of the day and often including Sunday.

Letters, Elton Lewis, Ex-Police Sergeant. In reply to Mr Kinkead, I say that no doubt the original idea behind the concessions there were well motivated, but it's not difficult for a visitor to discern that it has resolved itself into wholesale licence over the years. **Sooner or later, some authority will have to restrict the orgy.**

For too long, it has been the habit of politicians to pass on to police the strategy of "turning a blind eye" when an amendment to the law would be honest policy.

Letters, S Bailey. What of the women of Broken Hill? Have they been invited to express their views? It may be taken for granted that they have very decided opinions about beer being available "round the clock" and about unlimited facilities to gamble, to say nothing of the example set the hordes of children, who are not unobservant.

Are not the women worthy of more consideration than any other section of any community? I insist there is not a "mother's son" who does the same remarkable job as a housewife where there are children to attend to. It is an everyday task over 10 to 12 hours to which the basic wage and penalty rates do not apply!

Against that, the "lord and master" – at Broken Hill, anyway – does at most a 40-hour week, and with the air of a martyr, feels that he is entitled to special drinking privileges. What a set-up it would be if the womenfolk did the same kind of thing!

Whatever claims the men of Broken Hill imagine they may have for an easing of trading hours, they are not differently placed to thousands of others in the north and north-west of this State in such towns as Bourke, Brewarrina, Nyngan, Cobar, Narrandera, Hay, and scores of smaller places.

In any case, surely the interests of women and children come first. What do they wish?

Letters, A Master. I am sorry the dear lady S Bailey could not be invited to express her views. The poor martyr seems to have done well in any case.

Letters, Mary Guilda, Broken Hill. I would like to take issue with Mrs Bailey. She is more concerned with being the housewife martyr than with the truth.

Let me illustrate with my husband, who incidentally does not gamble. He is one of a hundred men who work in a mine, and who work one month on dog-watch out of every three months. That means, six days a week, he goes down the mine at 10 in the evening and comes up at six in the morning. There is an hour's travel each way in company busses.

He comes home and sleeps six hours. If he then wants a beer, he can't have one, because at work he is sniffed for alcohol, because of underground security reasons.

It works out that the only time he can drink is on Saturday night. Then the pubs are supposed to be shut. This might please Mrs Bailey, but it's a scandal.

Mrs Bailey is happy in her world, changing a few nappies every day, and complaining to her hairdresser about how hard she works. But these men actually do hard Labor, in a putrid mine, eight hours a day, for six days a week. It is a bad society that will not let them have a beer on the only night in the week that they can.

The same applies to most of the men in Broken Hill, one way or another.

DRAUGHT HORSES VERSUS MOTORS

Letters, William Tremain. All political parties are appealing for more production of wheat. I consider that the decline has been brought about to a large extent by the replacement of the draught horse by mechanical power and motors.

The small grower who at one time produced a good percentage of the wheat crop is now eliminated. At one time, about 11 years ago, wheat was produced to such an extent (and in this district practically all by horse-teams) that it was necessary to put the growers on a quota system as they were producing more wheat than could be handled.

In my opinion, if the Government stopped the slaughter of good draught horses and the landowners co-operated by using horses, there would be an increase in wheat production. There are plenty of young men willing to grow wheat with horse teams, who could do well for themselves and the landowner on a share basis, but who have not the large amount of money necessary to buy plant for mechanical production of wheat.

Letters, G Hardman. Taxation and the high cost of production contribute more to the lowering of wheat yields than the change from horse to mechanical power. As for the small grower, there is no reason why he should not use horsepower (animal type).

A large amount of time and land is taken up for the purpose of growing feed for the draught horse, whereas with tractors, "feed" may be obtained from drums.

The suggestion that there are plenty of young men wiling to grow wheat with horse teams is debatable. I have not met very many willing to do so. The old grey mare just isn't what she used to be.

Letters, R Sweeney, Cootamundra. It was pleasing to see someone had the courage to say a word in favour of the draught horse, and so I read with pleasure Mr Tremain's letter.

For a long time I have thought mechanisation of farming in a wholesale manner came to this young country too soon. Tractors and everything they devour had to be bought overseas, whereas 20 acres of oaten hay and a similar area of oats stripped for grain would keep two teams of plough horses in ample feed. And two teams could put more land under crop than many of the tractors do today.

Of course, you need an extra man with horses. But isn't that all to the good?

America made her own tractors and had everything they needed to put in them, also a large population to feed; so it was natural she should turn to mechanisation of farming.

But we in Australia had ample land to graze horses when they were not working. They did the land more good than harm, and what was more pleasing than a couple of mares with foals at foot running in a little paddock near the homestead?

NEWS AND VIEWS

Letters, N H Hungerford. Some years ago my property was infested with red-back spiders, till a child got bitten by one.

I then allowed the fowls to roam round and underneath the house. Since then I have not seen a spider of any sort within three feet of the ground. The chooks got the lot, and still continue to keep the place free of spiders, snails, grubs, and most other pestiferous insects, except ants. All that remain are a few tree spiders which are harmless.

Letters, E Ripper. How long are we to have the farce of egg and milk advertising?

Surely there is no necessity to waste money in promoting sales of two such essential commodities. People are crying out for better supplies of both, but cannot afford them.

Many people who, in the past, never went without a breakfast egg are now obliged to economise. For such people to be urged to "eat more eggs" is absurd.

Letters, Linda Loneragan. One hears on all sides lately of the shortage of horses in Australia, yet over the last few years they have been rounded up in thousands, driven to the trucking yards, entrained to the cities – **thence to knackeries to feed coursing dogs**.

What is more, the conditions of travelling of Australian stock for market are unbelievable in their cruelty. It is a blot on our national **education**, both religious and secular.

One wishes the RSPCA had a powerful backing by town and country.

Letters, P Alley. Country people in outside areas are much perturbed at the prospect of the Government spending huge sums on TV whilst they have to put up with indifferent phone services. Better phones, good roads, and cheaper transport are all essential. TV is not nearly so necessary.

MARCH: PAINLESS CHILDBIRTH?

In the years around 1930, an English doctor, Grantly Read, made a name for himself by writing and talking about a method he pioneered for **reducing pain for mothers in child birth**. The NSW Health Department had picked up his ideas, and had been advocating them since 1938. By 1953, the idea was gaining popularity here in Australia, and was more and more becoming a matter for discussion.

Dr Read's main doctrine was that the pain is chiefly caused by fear, and a resulting state of tension in the mother that obstructs the delivery of the baby. An important part of his programme was the giving of talks to mothers on the physiology of pregnancy and birth, so that what happens to them **would not have the terrors of the unknown**.

Of course, in the year 2020 everyone is familiar with these concepts, and prenatal classes are held regularly all over the place. But in 1953, the ideas were novel, and perhaps the most common way to reduce pain was by anaesthetics. In those days, that meant that the mother-to-be was knocked out for a substantial period of time, and hopefully, when she awoke, the whole process was over. My own wife was born under this regime in 1951, and her mother did not see her for thirty hours after the birth.

Subsequently, chemically induced spinal blocks took over from anaesthetics, and Caesarians have gradually become more common. In any case, though, back in 1953, the Read method was under the microscope.

Letters, G Fowler. On my baby's birthday I asked a maternity hospital sister to examine me and was shocked by her reply: "You're nowhere near ready for the Labor Ward if you can still smile."

The misplaced pity of fellow-patients was bad enough; but to have this said by a woman trained in midwifery reflected shame on our national ignorance.

As a mother, I condemn the belief that painful birth is natural. Thousands of women in many countries – but, unfortunately, few in our own – know birth as a joyful experience, of which they would not want to be robbed by the use of anaesthetics. Anaesthetics are essential, when there is pain, but I look forward to the day when they will be necessary only in a rare emergency.

Every day in our maternity hospitals women suffer unnecessarily. Pain in birth is caused by expecting it. I earnestly recommend anyone interested in breaking out of this medieval darkness to read *Natural Childbirth* by G D Read, an English doctor.

I enjoyed having my baby, and if those who were supposed to help me had refrained from telling me how painful it should have been, I would have enjoyed it more.

Letters, G B Treacy.   At one of my early prenatal visits to the doctor, I asked for information on Labor relaxation methods, but was told not to worry about such things just yet, and that everything would be taken care of at the time.

After my arrival at the Labor Ward, my confidence melted away when I was left alone for hours on end, with no explanations. The anaesthetics I was given later were administered without prior consultation.

Not every type of woman is capable of undergoing painless childbirth, but those who wish to help themselves should be encouraged to do so. The doctor who has the patience and inclination to talk the subject over is indeed a rare find.

Letters, Blessed Oblivion. If Mrs Fowler is one of those fortunates who can dispense with the merciful help of anaesthetics, then good luck to her. But why this outburst because she was offered sympathy?

I have had two children. Whereas the second experience was like a painful dream, which is now forgotten, the first was a terrible nightmare which I think will be with me forever.

I will leave Mrs Fowler to the perusal of G D Read, but she must leave me the anaesthetics.

Letters, Yvonne C Farmer. Both Mrs Fowler and Mrs D Hill, writing of their experience in following Dr Reade's book, give the impression to the public that nursing staffs were both surprised and uncooperative in their efforts to carry out this method.

As a nursing sister in charge of a small obstetric unit, may I say that such is not always the case, and hasten to give a word of encouragement to expectant mothers who may have this fear. I would think that your correspondents attended large, busy hospitals and did not state their desires with enthusiasm.

Patients wishing to adopt this method are encouraged here, and excellent results have been experienced. I would like to suggest that expectant mothers really anxious to study and carry out painless childbirth select small hospitals, where there is more time for the personal element, and make known their desires some time before entering the hospital. It is then possible for all members of the staff to be prepared to give their fullest cooperation.

Letters, A Sanderson. Nurse Louise Robinson's remark that "doctors are too busy to instruct or teach expectant mothers" is perhaps the keynote to the whole problem of "unnatural" childbirth.

Dr Grantly Dick Read's wisdom and knowledge came from observations made at the bedside of a poverty-stricken woman. Her quiet trust in nature and the power of the mind over her body gave him the inspiration to work on his natural childbirth theory.

Medical science has not yet fully grasped the significance of the patient's confidence and peace of mind. The simple unhurried teaching of a family doctor can and often does contribute more to preventive medicine than elaborate equipment and expensive drugs.

Surely teaching should be a primary function of medical science.

Letters, Senior Maternity Nurse. I read with interest your Kiama correspondent who talked childbirth in country hospitals.

My own wide experience is that the Reade method is nothing but a nuisance. The women who use it want to be coddled and cajoled right throughout the birth process, and require one nurse to every patient. Often, at night I have to look after ten mothers-to-be. I have no time for their non-stop requests for more information and comforting words.

If they want to cut down on pain, anaesthetics are useful, they will probably miss out on the bits they would like to remember. My best advice is by all means study up on the physiology, but to accept the fact that no one can stop the pain and at the same time have you keep consciousness. Make your mind up, and stop bleating.

Comment. A few dozen writers were enthusiastic about Read's writings. You can see from the Letters that the use of the Read method was still in its infancy, and needed some selling.

GIVE WOMEN A BREAK

Not all women were having fun with childbirth. Letters from them kept popping up in the papers, asking for sensible changes to their status. These did not indicate a widespread agitation for the "Liberation" that was so earnestly sought in later decades, but it did signal that thoughtful writers were starting to push for deserved changes.

Letters, T J Ryan. Reference to the fine achievement of Miss Jean Austin in gaining prizes for general proficiency in third-year law prompts the question, has not the time come when talented women lawyers should be raised to the Bench?

To regard this as absurd would itself be absurd, because the only reason against it would be their sex. Legal knowledge and character alone qualify for the Bench, to which women would bring just as much legal learning and distinction as men.

Letters, Irene Connelly, United Associations of Women. T J Ryan poses a question often asked by visitors from countries where women Judges are a commonplace.

These visitors are equally amazed that rarely are our women barristers entrusted with briefs.

The answer that our association has always had to give to these questions has been that in Australia the highest qualifications are no match for prejudice.

In reply to the question: "Are we lacking in women who achieve distinction in their professions?" we can quote with justifiable pride such achievements as those of Miss Elizabeth Evatt and Miss Jean Austin.

In another column of the same issue the experiences of a woman doctor are related. They tell a similar story of sex bias – of applications for positions received with eagerness until it is found that the person applying is a woman.

Only when Australia can be induced to relinquish its custom of calling only upon the talents of half of its people, and when appointments are made on the qualifications and not on the sex of the person, can we claim to be a true democracy.

Letters, Alice Murphy. Sydney is shabbily treated as regards the provision of public telephone booths.

I have lived in five suburbs but the position is always the same. There may be three or four boxes in one district, widely scattered from one another. Or, in the rare event of there being two together, you may be sure one is out of order.

Each box has its queue, which can overhear every word spoken by the hapless person using the instrument. Quite often, overcome by the publicity, the impatient jingle of pennies, and the loud imprecations, I have come away from a box leaving my real reason for telephoning unspoken. And it is just too preposterous for words to hope to make more than one call. A person would have to be very thick-skinned to be so venturesome.

The general idea seems to be that women who use public phones are just wasting time chattering. Why should they be regarded as nuisances if they do? Housewives' horizons are limited enough, goodness knows. Why should it be considered so shocking if they spend some minutes on the phone talking to friends?

SCHOOLS OF ARTS

I spent the first 17 years of my life in a small coal-mining town in the Cessnock coalfields. It was a poor town of 2,000, where the level of education was low, and the middle class consisted of a handful of business people, a few mine managers, two policemen, a postmaster and a railway station master. The latter was very important, and was held in very high regard by himself and his family.

Right in the middle of Abermain was a large building that was conspicuous because it was built of brick. The only other such structures in town were the Police Station, and a Mines Rescue Station. This large structure was called a School of Arts, and this seemed remarkable, because it did nothing that was in any way scholarly, and it made no pretence of promoting arts in any form, or fostering interest in the arts.

In fact, it had a number of small rooms that were rarely used used for meetings, and one quite large room housed a library. But even within the library, there was no sign of erudition or of the arts. There were plenty, hundreds in fact, of American-style westerns, thirty Perry Masons, twenty Wodehouse with the inimitable Bertie and Jeeves. There were also thousands of "women's books", written before Mills and Boon got a big share of that market. And there were stacks of other books and comic books, not quite so high in literary value.

These Schools of Arts, I found out later, were widely spread throughout country towns and small cities, all across Australia. Any little population that had a big number of British migrants was liable to have its own School. Most of them in 1953 had degenerated, as in Abermain, into local libraries and meeting rooms. A few, like the one in adjacent Weston, also had a billiards room, and a single three-wheel fruit machine, and an SP bookie. They were mainly owned and funded by local Councils.

In 1953, the writing was on the wall for these Schools of Arts. This was sad in a way, because from the beginning of the Century, these Schools had provided basic education and focal points for expressions of the Arts, in communities that were very nearly illiterate. As education reached more and more people over a half-century, the need for them dropped quite a deal.

The correspondence below presents various aspects of their diminishing status.

Letters, Minerva. It would be interesting to know something of the origin and history of Schools of Arts and to consider whether an inquiry into their usefulness is not overdue.

Recently I visited a small but busy country town in Victoria, and I found the School of Arts housed in the municipal hall. It consisted of two large rooms – one a library containing thousands of ill-kept books, entirely unclassified.

The attendant on duty was more interested in running a billiards saloon attached to the so-called School of Arts than in caring for or servicing the library. He told me that a few new books were bought monthly, but these did not include technical books, for the local youth would not read them.

Another such school of culture I visited in Sydney was well kept, housed, and arranged, but consisted entirely of light fiction, comics, westerns, and detective literature. Another in a large centre in the Blue Mountains, though in charge of a pleasant young woman, was tragic in its low standard of literature.

Could not something be done to revitalise these centres, which should be the foundation of culture for young intelligent Australians?

Letters, Book Lover. Your correspondent's letter on schools of arts was timely.

The main Sydney School of Arts differs only in degree from those your correspondent mentions. There are the Westerns, comics, detectives and light romances which your correspondents saw in country areas – only more of them.

This school of arts has a long and proud history. Many of our leading citizens and cultural leaders in the past have been connected with it, and it is a great pity to see it so changed.

The general section is appalling. I do not know who chooses the books, but there is evidently a dog and horse lover among them. There are hundreds of books about these animals.

Westerns and detective novels may have their place, but not to the extent of crowding out good literature. Schools of arts today seem to be playing down to the lowest common taste, and it is insulting to be faced with row upon row of sterile, futile literature.

Letters, W Smith. A still greater need is the revival of the debating clubs which were so prominent and so popular some years ago. The School of Arts was then a cultural centre and the Government contributed a small subsidy.

Strong debating clubs were to be found in Sydney, at Randwick, Newtown, Ashfield, North Sydney and Chatswood. A challenge shield was given for annual competition and the lecture rooms were crowded for interclub debates, public lectures and literary nights.

Radio and the cinema have contributed to the decline of the School of Arts, but I would plead for a revival of interest in the oldest and perhaps greatest of "arts" – that of public speaking.

Schools of Arts committees, consisting of voluntary workers, will continue to struggle on, until the time comes when they are no longer needed. A School of Arts I have in mind is very proud of the fact that it is still able to serve the public as a friendly meeting place, and with a mixture of books they like to read.

Letters, Trustee. As a trustee of one of these bodies for many years, I feel they are now obsolete.

Formerly, in the suburbs, they were social centres with fine libraries, and the meeting place of citizens primarily interested in local civic welfare, from which future public men often graduated.

Many will recall the excellent inter-Schools of Art (or Literary Institute) debates in Sydney of over 30 years ago, with teams competing for a coveted shield.

Time has marched on.

Since the advent of "talkies" and the radio, public interest in Schools of Art has lapsed. Private local lending libraries appear now to cater for fiction lovers, while students' textbooks and research works are provided in the more complete Government or semi-Government libraries in the city.

A NOTE ON CAPTAIN COOK

Every now and then, in writing these books, I indulge myself one way or another. Right now, I intend to do just that. My only justification for that is the Letter below appeared in the *SMH* on March 27, **1953**. But somehow it seemed to me to be too good to keep to myself. So, for better or worse, here it is.

Letters, (Miss) G Paternoster, London. The article entitled "London's Australia" has just reached me in London, and being one of those 40,000 Australian in England during Coronation year, I was interested especially in the fact that it is stated that Captain James Cook "lived a happy married life blessed by six children."

Last week I went to Cambridge and discovered what I think is one of history's saddest but least known footnotes. There, in the centre aisle of the Church of St Andrew the Great, rests the bodies of Captain Cook's wife, Elizabeth Cook, and two of their sons. Of their six children, three had died in infancy and on Captain Cook's final visit home in 1776, when Hugh was born, Nathaniel and James were worrying their parents to enter the Navy.

So until 1780 Elizabeth Cook remained home alone, except for little Hugh, and eventually a message came that her husband had been killed 20 months before. In the same month as she received this news, further news came of Nathaniel's death in the West Indies. With Hugh growing up and a student at Christ's College, Cambridge, tragedy struck again, for on her wedding anniversary her beloved youngest son died. She and James (on leave from the Navy) attended the funeral service in the Church of St Andrew the Great. Within two weeks the sorrowing mother was there again – alone this time – for the funeral of James drowned in a high sea.

JOE STALIN'S DEATH

Letters, J W Downing. It was a pleasure to read your straight-speaking leading article about the late Joe Stalin's career, a Russian dictator, in contrast with all the dissimulation which is pouring out from politicians and others.

The degree to which modern society **has become corrupted** is shown by the fact that national leaders can find **complimentary things to say on the most evil men of history**. They apparently confuse the attainment of political power with spiritual merit, or forget that, as in the analogy your leading article draws, anyone sufficiently lacking in scruple can achieve almost any figure or power in the estimation of ignorant masses.

Let those who unctuously speak of Stalin's contribution to the "victory" of the Allies in World War II remember that Russia fought in her own defence, and raised not a finger for world liberty until she was betrayed in her unholy compact with Stalin's fellow-monster, Hitler.

Letters, G Hirst. Notwithstanding the statement that Mr Stalin's body was buried without religious rites, the *Herald* 10 contains a picture of Russians carrying huge wreaths of flowers on their way to the Hall of Columns in which Stalin's body was lying.

It would appear that there is a more widespread religious feeling in Russia than is supposed, or else a general ignorance of the meaning of the wreath – the victory over life – which the wreath commemorates and symbolises. To a non-religious society such as Communism, death is in no way a victory but something which terminates one's personal triumph in living.

REMEMBER MISTER WHIPPY?

Letters, R S Reid, JP. The interesting controversy created by the suggested transfer of the flying-boat base from Rose Bay should awaken in our authorities the will to control noise in general. Much of it is preventable.

It is waste of public funds to issue brochures on the effect of noise to health, if the local authorities and police will not enforce ordinances or a section of the Police Offences act, 1901-47, Section 9 of which reads:

"Whosoever in any street or public place blows any horn (unless he is a guard or postman in her Majesty's

Post Office in the performance of his duty), or uses any other noisy instrument for the purpose of announcing any show or entertainment, or for the purpose of hawking, selling, distributing, or collecting any article whatsoever, or of obtaining money or alms, shall be liable to a penalty not exceeding two pounds."

This on the face of it seems sufficient to stop all the noises that plague our existence. But its enforcement is another matter.

The public is not happy about the way Sunday is being used by the vendors of wares, some with raucous whistles and others with loud bells. The authorities would not be denying anyone a livelihood if the provisions of the Act were enforced.

NEWS AND VIEWS

Letters, Ivor Freshman. The last and only spot in the British Commonwealth of Nations where insanity is not a cause for divorce is New South Wales.

Mr P E Joske, member for Balaclava, has prepared a bill providing for the uniformity of divorce laws in the Commonwealth, and this is awaited with the keenest interest by many people, who are penalised morally, domestically and socially, because the other marriage partner is incurably insane.

It is to be hoped that Mr Joske will push ahead with his bill, or, alternatively, submit one pressing for the inclusion of the insanity clause in the divorce laws of New South Wales.

Letters, C Armstrong. In recent letters on the subject of fish conservation, the real cause of the falling off of the fish population was not mentioned. It is the extremely wasteful methods of licensed fishermen.

I have seen many nets "shot." They are dragged up on the beach and a fisherman goes from one wing end to the other, picking out the legal-length fish. In the case of a small net, say 400 yards, this will take about half an hour. The net is then tipped over to spill out the small fish, porcupines, shellfish and seaweed, which are left to rot and pollute the beach.

In a good haul from Lake Macquarie,100 small bream, whiting or schnapper are killed for every edible fish taken. No net should be hauled to the beach in the absence of a fishing inspector, and extravagant fishermen should be delicensed.

Letters, Clarice McNamara. Parents should be the best sex educators, but it is common knowledge that many parents fail in this, as in many other important parental duties, because their own attitude towards sex is unhealthy or because they simply do not know how to answer the child's early questions.

The problem should be tackled in two ways: First by the widespread provision of the sort of education which helps intending parents and parents to understand the emotional as well as physical development and needs of the normal child; secondly, by training teachers in training colleges and through refresher courses to supplement the sex education begun at home.

Letters, Fairplay. Mr C A Hungerford, writing of the koala, said: "It has never to my knowledge been killed in any numbers by white people."

During the depression of the early thirties, the Queensland Government declared an open season for the koala to assist the people of that State to earn some sort of a living from the skins. The result was that more than **1,000,000 skins were taken** in a very short time, and that was not the only total by a long way.

APRIL: HOPE IN KOREA? MAYBE

Over the last few months, two important events might have changed the stalemate in Korea. Firstly, Harry Truman had been replaced by Eisenhower as President of the US. Then, Joseph Stalin, boss-man of the Communist state in Russia, had died. That meant that in both countries, old policies were being re-evaluated, and there was a change in the management at the top. There was considerable world-wide speculation that maybe both parties, the Communists and the Capitalists, would bury their ideological war, and make genuine efforts for peace – at last.

I remind you that the most apparent obstacle to peace was a dispute over what to do with Prisoners-Of-War. Each of the two parties now held over 100,000 POWs in captivity, and the argument was about how a formula for repatriation would work. Over the last year, neither side had shown the least bit of urgency over this matter, and both had done their best to frustrate any chance of finding a solution.

Now, however, with changes at the top, maybe things might get better. In early April, it was suggested that the wounded and ill prisoners from both sides could be swapped. To the surprise of the entire world, this new policy was adopted, and believe it or not, within the month, about 650 UN POWs had been released, and the same number of Reds.

On top of that, the Reds and the UN-USA agreed that full armistice talks should now resume after months of stalling. And by then, fighting in the war had almost come to a standstill. There was a distinct possibility that peace could break out at any time, though there were many cynics who thought they detected a false dawn. **Time will tell.**

THE WAR IN AUSTRALIA

In April when 1,000 Korean veterans returned from overseas and marched through Brisbane, 60,000 people turned out to cheer them. In Sydney, a few days later, the crowd was 100,000. There was no doubt that the Oz men fighting the war had the full nation's support. **But the war itself was quite unpopular.** Some people, who had been against Australia sending troops in the first place, still argued that this was just a civil war between the North and the South of Korea. What did it have to do with us, and why should we send our young men to get killed there? Others argued that it was just a showpiece war, where the two great ideologies of the world could flex their muscles on neutral territory, and make much propaganda out of it. But the majority of folk were just tired of it, and saw it as completely fruitless and that it was solving nothing. They just wanted it to end, and our boys to come home.

At this stage, a **few** people got their wish. A **handful of Australians** were released in the current prisoner swap. Sadly, a lot more remained in captivity.

SHAKESPEARE IN SYDNEY

There was much excitement near the Tivoli Theatre in Sydney. The hallowed Stratford-upon-Avon Memorial Theatre Company, from the hunting ground of Shakespeare himself, was about to open a nine-week season in Sydney. They intended to present just three plays, *Othello, As You Like It,* and *Henry IV.* On the first day of ticket sales, a queue started to develop at 4.40am, and by the time the box office opened, it had grown to 100, mostly women. Throughout the day it was kept steady at 70, though it grew to 250 between 5 and 6 pm. There was the normal number of people who fainted during the waiting.

Comment. The season was a huge success. I saw two of the plays at the behest of a beautiful red-headed lass, who had much more culture than I ever had. But I came away a bit less of a philistine than I had been before, though my school-boy biases took a lot of shifting

Comments of Others. Mr Anthony Quale, Director of the tour, had his views on the teaching of Shakespeare. He described as "terrible" the present school methods of parsing and analysing Shakespeare's works. He believed that there were **three good reasons** why a great number of persons had no appreciation of Shakespeare.

"**The first** is the fear that they lack the training to understand him – that they are uneducated," he said. "**The second** is the prejudice against Shakespeare that has come from the terrible methods of teaching him in schools.

"Shakespearean plays are full of mature adult human observation and situation. Shakespeare wrote for grown men and women. He was extremely uninhibited, and his plays are filled with episodes of murder, violence and lust that should not be thrust down the gullets of schoolchildren.

"Children just don't understand. I myself at the age of 14 had to learn the soliloquy, 'To Be Or Not To Be,' and I didn't understand it. How was I to know, at that age, what it meant for a man to be so distraught by worry that he could be on the verge of suicide? How can a child understand that children make fun of a man who is mad, and only when they grow older do they appreciate that madness is not a comedy, it is a tragedy.

"When you attempt to drum Shakespeare into schoolchildren, you run the risk of turning Shakespeare, in their imaginations, into the same thing as syrup of figs, and driving them away from him for the rest of their lives."

The third reason why many people did not like Shakespeare was that individuals who posed as experts on music, art and literature had made him their pet.

"The ordinary person tends to say: 'These people don't seem to me to be very admirable people, therefore what they like can't be very admirable either'," he said.

"This again is ironic, because this type of people is the type Shakespeare in his own day turned his back upon."

Letters, M C. If Mr Anthony Quayle can find a school in NSW which teaches appreciation of Shakespeare by the "terrible" method of parsing and analysing his works, I'll buy him a ticket for one of his own performances.

Performing the plays studied has been the usual practice for years, even in schools (and they are many) that have neither stages nor assembly halls.

I have seen schoolgirls of average intelligence present Shakespeare under a tree in the playground, with a freshness and spontaneity rarely equalled and never surpassed by adult amateurs.

Letters, Glossary. In my High school association with Shakespeare, I parsed and analysed his works until I was sickened. Never once was the beauty of the plays emphasised. They became merely skeletal structures of words.

As for playing Shakespeare, we did – once. And that was a piece from "A Midsummer Night's Dream," which is tinkered with by everyone. All students in the play hated every bit of it.

WARNING: THE CORONATION IS COMING

This warning will mean nothing to those of you who like to catch the British Royals. But there are many people who, while wishing well to these stellar people, would like to not be fed Royal exploits for weeks on end during supposedly festive occasions. For those people, let me say that you are about to be deluged by a mass of media, the like of which you have never seen before. To be a bit more specific, Princess Elizabeth will be crowned as Queen of England and the Empire, in a ceremony at Westminster Abbey in June. I intend to cover the event, but sparingly.

In the meantime, various bodies here in Oz are gearing up for the occasion. A few have already made their mark in the local Letters column.

Letters, (Mrs) A Morrisey, NSW War Widows' Guild. As all sections of the community are being represented at the Coronation, we are deeply grieved that the Commonwealth Government has not invited a woman to represent the 10,000 War widows throughout Australasia.

To all women in Australia the crowning of a Queen has a special personal and spiritual significance. It is sad that the chief mourners of the men who gave their lives for their country are not being represented at the Coronation which will consecrate not only a young Sovereign to the service of her subjects, but the subjects themselves in fealty and allegiance to her person.

Comment. The Government pointed out that there were several War widows invited to many functions, and that they would be given a preferred place at all ceremonies. The wrong impression had been gained by the writer because there had been delays in acceptances by the women, and the Government could not publish lists until the names were in.

Letters, H E Shying. Who will be representing at the Coronation those men and women so often referred to as "Our Glorious Dead"?

I do not wish to be told that some Service officer or parliamentarian is representing our lost ones unless such person has been one who has suffered the loss of a beloved child.

Could we not send from each State the parents of someone who laid down his or her life so that this great country could survive?

In London, the action was really starting to heat up. For example, it appears that the price of seats on the coronation route had been slipping. They started at 42 Pounds each, and were now down to 27 Pounds. On top of that, buyers were being offered breakfast, a champagne lunch, afternoon tea, and a televised broadcast of the event. The more expensive seats in a window seat in Oxford Street will cost 79 Pounds. Rents, however, had risen to rather high levels. For example, the weekly price of a Kensington house was 525 Pounds.

Comment. Behind these superficialities, the planning for the coronation was proceeding nicely, for what was certain to be a huge and spectacular event.

SHOWGROUND COCKY, 45, IS MISSING

The overseer of the Sydney Show Ground, RAS, Mr Sid Haron, appealed last night to the person who took his 45-year-old white cockatoo from the Showground on Saturday to feed the bird on grilled chops and milk.

"Because of his age he has to have a special diet," said Mr Haron. "I am afraid he will die if he doesn't get his chops and milk."

Mr Haron is offering a reward for the cockatoo, which has a very extensive vocabulary, sings, and answers to the name of Cocko. The bird has perched on the fence between the Sydney Cricket Ground and the Showground every day since 1939.

He was on a chain attached to the fence when he was stolen on Saturday. Mr Haron said the bird would not sleep at night unless placed in a paper bag.

Police Report, April 8th. Cocko, the 45 year-old cockatoo, was found yesterday by police. He was found in a suburban back-yard after an anonymous phone call. His owner, Sid Haron, said that he received numerous phone calls after news of his disappearance was published.

"He came back in the police car, strutting up and down on the back seat. When he got back in the house, he went nearly mad. He has been dancing around, flapping his wings and calling out for my daughter ever since he got home." After a meal of grilled chop, washed down with milk, Cocko walked into his paper bag, and soon went to sleep.

THOUGHTS ON TODAY'S CHILDREN

I suppose that after seven years of Baby Boom you should expect that the roles and rights of children would come up for discussion. Many writers – inevitably – claimed that the children of today were badly behaved compared to previous generations. On the other hand, there was a smaller number of correspondents who found some virtue in the little blighters. Below, I mainly reflect the views of the latter writers.

Letters, R Kellett. The subject of child misbehavior referred to by M E A Gee is important.

The reading of "comics" featuring violence, and seeing films suitable only for adults, have a bad effect.

Recently I attended a bitterly contested boxing contest (my only visit). Almost at my elbow a boy in his early teens kept continuously shouting, "Knock his block off." When I asked him to go easy, he glowered and changed to, "Knock his brains out," which he repeated until his voice failed. Near him was a girl, quite amused by the boy, and herself also shouting.

One wonders what the result of this lack of restraint and discipline among our young people will be.

Letters, J H Moore. Recent correspondence about the behavior of children on trams and other places suggests that many adults resent children and why is this so?

Is it because we are selfish and think only of our own comfort? Or is it because we feel that children are inferior to us sophisticated and superior adults?

Children by their animated spirits, their refreshing keenness, their freedom from bigotry, hatred and malice, shame our adult sloth, apathy and rancour.

Let us throw off puritanical Victorianism, with its platitudes which have failed to make the world a better place, and come to realise that children have a right to be treated by adults as we would that they, in similar circumstances, would treat us.

Letters, Ruth Bedford. Certainly children have their rights, among them the right of being brought up to be healthy, happy and useful citizens – but this involves consideration of others.

Parents today are often too overworked and tired to teach a child the lessons that only a parent can properly teach. No one who loves and understands children can view without dismay the inconsiderate behaviour one sees far too often, or fail to grieve for the children themselves who need the uncaring but wise guidance they have a right to expect. Children respect authority.

Divorce courts and criminal courts are full of unhappy people who have never been taught that "What I want" must be adjusted, to a reasonable extent, to what other people want.

Letters, L M Thomas. Please allow me space to endorse the sentiments of J H Moore on children.

As a very recent visitor to the city of Sydney, one of my main impressions was the readiness children displayed in giving their seats to their elders, and always with a smile. I had occasion to cross Edgecliff Road, Woollahra, one Sunday evening on my way to church, and a little boy about eight years old, noticing my hesitancy, came to my assistance, placed his hand under my elbow, and helped me across. I was most impressed.

Letters, Neil Grace. Some people seem to enjoy advocating "strict discipline" in child training. I fear they love their own power far more than they love youngsters. They would rather see servility than self-reliance in the young.

We should admire the parents who give advice rather than commands, and those who enjoy the confidence of their children instead of a negative fearful "respect."

Letters, Vera Macmillan. After reading Colonel Llewellyn's candid article on our standards of riding at the Show, may I be permitted to speak on behalf of the children – particularly in jumping events?

What the Colonel says is true. Since I gave up active riding, I have been judging in many Shows and it has been evident to me that the children are not schooled enough in horsemanship. They are not altogether to blame, as jumping for juvenile riders is still in its infancy at the RAS, and very few agricultural shows put on classes to encourage them. The fences are too small and, instead of this making for safety (which, I think, was the intention of the RAS), the ponies take liberties with them and tear round at a gallop. Also the judges usually demand a dashing display, which is so bad for both horse and rider.

There are a number of us who would be delighted to give our time to improve our young riders and make us proud of them.

WHAT ABOUT A KB OR TWO?

Letters, O Piggott, NSW Temperance Society. You published figures on Australia's liquor consumption with a commentary that glorified the nation for its high consumption of beer.

I want to point out that behind this great expenditure of money stands the spectre of sorrow, misery, insanity, and crime.

Letters, Chesney Harte, Royal Blind Society. Are we to be proud of our beer-drinking record? What is the record of deaths of innocent people killed by motorists driving under its influence, in addition to the many thousands injured?

Where is the record of broken homes bringing distress and poverty to wife and little children? Where is the record for drunkenness and the cost in dealing with them?

Letters, Bruce Dalton. I can assure Rev Chesney Harte that I for one am terribly ashamed of our beer drinking record. The fact that my fellow Australians prefer watery, rancid beer to the glorious wines of their own country seems to me almost beyond belief.

It is a dreadful thing that the charms of Chablis, the beauties of Burgundy or the subtleties of sherry mean nothing to the great majority.

Letters, Ernest Drinker. I do not like the way the clergy and others have been abusing all and sundry. I like to drink a moderate amount of beer. But, I assure your clergy, I do not kill people on the roads, I have a happy home-life, and a loving wife and children, and I am never drunk, nor am I charged with drunkenness. Then again, I am not miserable, sorrowful or insane. None of my family are, either.

I like beer as it is. I do not find it watery, nor rancid. If **you** do, I don't mind if you drink wine, but I won't tell you that somehow you are thereby doing the wrong thing. And you should leave me alone and let me drink what I want.

Really, I do not need your advice.

Comment. Wine consumption at the time was mainly of fortified wines. So, consumption figures for ports and sherries and muscats were fairly high. Table wines were still foreign to most Australians.

For public transport travellers at night, the sight they dreaded was an approaching man carrying a brown paper bag, and having the feeling that a half empty bottle of brown muscat was in it. If he sat down beside you, and gregariously offered you a swig, it left you with quite a dilemma. The only way out was to curl up and die.

DO WE LOVE THE JAPS YET?

Letters, R Gregory, 2/1 A A Regt Association. Peace has been officially signed at last with Japan, and its Ambassador is with us for Anzac Day for the first time since the War.

This may be necessary. However, let it be known far and wide that Diggers do not want his participation in any Anzac Day Service, and if this is classed as typical Australia bluntness, then let's be blunt.

Letters, W Johnston. Re the attendance of the Japanese Ambassador at Anzac Day celebrations, I say that surely it would be better to have Japanese taking part in Anzac Day, and making that day not merely a day of maudlin sentiment, and drinking, but rather a day of reminder of the horrors of war, and the sin of nationalism, and the need for real peace.

The way that many irresponsibles, under cover of the RSL, are treating and mis-using Anzac Day is increasingly making the day into one that decent citizens are finding objectionable.

Letters, An Elephant. About ten years ago, I was on Central Station as a trolley-load of Japanese Prisoners of War went past me on their way, I believe now, to Bowral. They were just babies, not yet in their twenties. They were chained together, they were miserable and bewildered and hopeless. Their uniforms were filthy and torn, and so were their bodies. They looked like they would rather be dead.

A crowd of us gathered round them, and just looked at them. As they drew slowly away, the crowd, 100 of us, stared at the thirty of them, and not one word of sympathy was uttered. In fact, mumbles from many spectators indicated quite the contrary.

At the time, I felt no sympathy for them. Since then, I have not changed my mind. Some of my family were killed by them, and other friends imprisoned. Nothing has happened to make me think that they would not do the same again.

The two nations might be at peace, but to many of us, **we will never again be at peace.**

Comment. Australia was only eight years away from the end of WWII, and most people were not yet in a frame of mind to forgive or forget. Some people who lost family in the War would live the rest of their lives still burning with resentment against the Japanese.

On the other hand, there was a small but slowly-growing number of people who were saying it was about time we lived in the world as it currently was, and that meant putting aside all the iniquities of the past.

However, if the matter had been put to a vote, I hazard a guess that Mr Gregory's call for Japanese exclusion would have been upheld by quite a majority.

NEWS AND VIEWS

News item, April 24. Train travellers waiting at Hendra, Brisbane, were amazed today to see the normal steam train arriving at the station with a woman clinging to the front of the engine, looking very wind-blown.

Mrs Riordan of Clayfield had been using the level crossing at Clayfield, half a mile away, when she was struck by the train and caught on its cowcatcher. Her groceries went flying and her meat, but she managed to keep her umbrella, which was hooked over her arm.

She said she felt a little foolish. "For two minutes, I clung on. The speed of the train forced me back against the cowcatcher and stopped me from falling down in front of the wheels. When I got off the engine and told the driver I had been there since Clayfield, you could have knocked his eyes off with a stick."

Letters, QX4219, AIF. English and New Zealand racing clubs had the good taste to abandon their race meetings for the day following the death of King George VI. Australian clubs held their programmes as usual.

Now, Sydney and Newcastle clubs have seized on yet another day of national mourning on which to hold race meetings – a full programme of races is set down for Anzac Day. While certain war charities are said to benefit from the Anzac Day meetings, there are other Saturday meetings which could benefit these causes.

Letters, Stamp Dealer. The Postmaster-General is very active in his efforts to enlist the aid of philatelists in boosting the Commonwealth revenue.

His efforts are surely discounted by the action of his colleague, the Minister of Trade and Customs, who by import restrictions curtails the pursuit of this fascinating hobby.

The writer is a small dealer among juvenile and primary stamp collectors, and has been in the habit of importing stamps from London. He is now informed that this educational hobby is a "non essential" and that no import licences can be issued for the purpose of importing foreign stamps. I suggest that more latitude could be shown to the dealer in stamps whose comparatively minor imports would not seriously inconvenience the Australian economy.

MAY: IT'S ALL QUITE A CIRCUS

News item, Coffs Harbour, May 26. Three fully-grown lions were wandering this small coastal city this afternoon after escaping from their Wirth's Circus. An elephant was also on the loose. They escaped as their cages were crossing a railway line in the Coffs Harbour Yards when an engine hit them. The cage was damaged and the lions escaped through the twisted bars. The elephant got excited and broke away from his harness.

The population of the city and the surrounding neighbourhood have been told by the police to stay indoors. Reinforcement police have been drafted from nearby city of Grafton. "Police are carrying .303 rifles and intend to shoot if the lions attack. Roadblocks have been set up round the city to warn and perhaps deter travellers."

New item, Coffs Harbour, May 27. The four animals that escaped from Wirth's Circus yesterday were re-captured today. The adventure with the three lions was a long and difficult operation.

After spending the night frightened and locked indoors, Mrs Wisely, a fisherman's wife, heard a disturbance in the fowl yard at the rear of their home. When she went outside to investigate, she found her chooks dead, and a lion in the yard. She screamed and went inside. Mr Wisely went outside, saw a large lion, and wisely retreated.

The lion was seen and surrounded by armed men. They re-constructed a big metal cage, and arranged nets strategically. After much whipping and prodding by the circus lion-tamer, this lion and another were driven into the cage.

A third lion made a noise at the tent door of an Aboriginal woman, Mrs Mercy, about midnight. She had been awakened, she thought, by her husband coming home. Instead, she looked up to see a lion in the doorway of her tent. Fortunately, the fabric of the tent was rotting, so she was able to tear her way out, and thus escape.

The lion then took refuge under a truck, and was taken by police in the morning.

The elephant was not so lucky. She was found badly injured in the near foreleg and hind leg, and had a deep gash in her hind quarters. The pad of her forefoot and parts of her two toes were torn off. A veterinary surgeon called to the scene thought that she could be saved. A woman attendant said she was in severe pain, and frequently wiped huge tears from the elephant's eyes.

Letters, A De Manchaux. Surely the most pathetic reading in today's "Herald" was the account of the escape and recapture of three lions, to say nothing of an elephant. The Sydney office of the RSPCA is being inundated with letters and telephone calls protesting against these noble but terrified animals being chased in fear of their lives – therefore endangering the lives of the public.

The idea of wild animals is supposed to give circus patrons a thrill – but does it? This form of "entertainment" with the exhibition of closely caged animals in travelling menageries is out of date and definitely cruel. Circus owners would be well advised to realise this and keep solely to the other more entertaining items on their programmes.

Letters, P Bennett. My reaction on reading of the escaped lions was a devout wish that they would be shot and put out of their misery.

How civilised human beings can bear the thought of these magnificent creatures housed in small cages with barely enough room to walk is a mystery. We permit this outrage and still try to teach our children to be kind to animals. No intelligent person can believe that wild beasts can be trained to do their silly tricks by kindness.

My son was taken with an art class to paint the lions at a circus, but he left without doing so. He said the look of sadness in their eyes was unbearable.

Letters, M Rathbone. I have yet to see anything more pathetic than the picture in the "Herald" of the lion which escaped from a circus. The poor beast was obviously more scared and panic stricken than its arms-laden hunters.

Modern entertainments are many and varied, so there should be no need for the imprisonment of wild beasts to amuse people. Children of to-day have many delights provided which constitute no cruelty or suffering, so why perpetuate this animal slavery?

Letters, N C M Skinner. Tuesday's high adventure of the Coffs Harbour hunters underlines the depravity of the Australian public conscience.

On top of the Coffs Harbour proceedings, we read of a lyrebird which was so confused or stupidly trusting as to enter a backyard at Gordon, and has been confined in the Zoo, presumably to remain there until its death. Again it seems that certain South Coast residents propose next Tuesday to honour their Queen's Coronation by, among other things, staging (and not for the first time, either), a contest in which humans will chase fowls in order to amuse other humans. Bravo.

Letters, G Large. People who write after the Coffs Harbour incident often deliberately confuse two arguments. There is **the first argument** that says that there is a risk to personal safety in maintaining ferocious animals. My answer is that of course there is, but it is trivial. They are confined in specially constructed cages, and handled with the utmost respect for safety. The fact of one incident in twenty years at Coffs Harbour should not be used to scare people.

The second argument is about the principle of keeping such animals in captivity. I acknowledge that this is undesirable, but as with so many things, you must weigh up the pros and cons. Against the discomfort of 1,000 animals Australia-wide being caged, you should weigh up the hundreds of thousands of people who visit the circus every year, and really get a thrill out of it. If you took away the animals, circuses would die.

Surely these people have the right to see a circus if they want to. Not only do animals have rights and freedoms. So do humans. We should not let the tail wag the donkey.

ELIZABETH'S CROWNING GLORY

There seems to be no doubt about it. The Coronation of Queen Elizabeth will go ahead next month. I suppose it will come to you as no shock to find that the City of London will react with all the pomp and ceremony they can muster, and that millions of people from all over the world will attend somewhere near, and that well-dressed people and horses will add glamour to the occasion. For my part, I will look to a few quirky bits to report.

Letters, H Sumpter. May I suggest that it would be unwise to hold any official Coronation Australian celebrations on the night of June 2. Surely a substantial number of people will wish to remain in-doors to listen to the broadcast from London, which will start at 8 p.m. EST.

Letters, Mary Booth, Anzac Fellowship of Women.
It comes as a great shock to learn that the Sydney Harbour fireworks display on Coronation night has been arranged at the very hour when, in Westminster Abbey, the great ceremony of dedication by the Queen is about to begin.

Here, surely, **is the moment for prayer by Australians** for her Majesty. Nothing would so bring home to us a sense of unity – to the younger generation it might well be a lifelong inspiration for loyalty and service.

The solemn proceedings of the Coronation should be broadcast by amplifiers in Hyde Park so that thousands of citizens, likely to be wandering about, can congregate and be at one in heart and mind with their fellow subjects.

Letters, D Gibson. I would like to know if the City of Sydney is doing anything to perpetuate the memory of the Coronation. I suppose that 300,000 Pounds will be spent on crackers, which are not appropriate for the coronation of a Queen.

Could not a fund be opened to set up some sort of permanent memorial of this great occasion.

Letters, Francis Everingham. Our elected Members in Federal Parliament are to receive fifty Shillings a day allowance while in Canberra for the Coronation celebrations in the capital.

Parliament will be in recess, and our Members will be engaged in the arduous occupation of eating and drinking at Commonwealth functions and listening to symphony concerts. They will be paid guests and not paying guests, and must earn nothing but contempt from the taxpayers of the Commonwealth.

Letters, JLM. Very many homes is Sydney have sets of small coloured electric lamps used on Christmas trees. It these were to be connected up on front porches, verandahs, etc, during Coronation week, what a pleasant effect could be obtained. Thousands of households would thus make their contribution to the illumination of our city.

Letters, TRADITIONALIST. As a general rule, traditions are a pleasant link with the past, but there is one tradition we could well do without, that **is the remission of prison sentences**, and sometimes amnesties, that are generally given as the triumphant ending of a war or as at present, the Coronation of a Sovereign. Society does not need these.

It is galling to think thieves, rogues, and swindlers, most of whom did not help win the War, and who have not served the Crown as good citizens, should be the persons who benefit most from such an historic and important occasion.

News item. The BBC hopes that Russia will stop jamming BBC shortwave stations on Coronation Day, so that a world-wide broadcast of the ceremony and procession will reach the Pacific and Far East without interference.

Russia has agreed to similar requests by the B.B.C. twice before, during broadcasts of the funerals of King George VI and Queen Mary.

The BBC Senior Superintendent yesterday said "We are hoping that with the publicity being given to the Coronation, the Russians will realise that on June 2 we shall not be worrying about sending them political talks.

He said that the BBC would broadcast a description of the Coronation service and procession in 44 languages. It would be relayed by at least 1,000 stations throughout the world.

FACTS ABOUT ABORIGINAL LIFESTYLE

Children of the Waste Land was apparently a 20-minute documentary film commissioned by a Church group. It showed Aboriginal living conditions, and the problems that they faced in a white-man's society.

The Letters below are included because they make clear the differences that existed, within Australia, regarding the "problem of Aborigines". On the one hand, there was the **strict Government line that everything possible was being done to help them**, and it was all working very well. If it was not going fast enough, it was because of the Aborigines themselves.

On the other hand, there was a small but growing number of people who were ashamed of the treatment and rules and prohibitions imposed on Aborigines, and wanted official recognition that major changes were immediately necessary.

Letters, H V Howe. Apparently the Chief Secretary's Department and the Commonwealth Film Censor have arrogated to themselves the power to curtail freedom of speech in Australia if such speech enunciates historical facts which offend their susceptibilities.

Their ban on the documentary film, "Children of the Waste Land," surely exceeds the limit of public tolerance of official suppression of truth and free speech.

The sooner "an unfortunate impression" is created at home and abroad, the better it will be for the few thousand surviving Aborigines in the Commonwealth. It is to be hoped the Chief Secretary's Department and the Commonwealth Film Censor will be forced to revoke the ban and that the script as spoken by the Bishop of

North Queensland will so arouse public opinion as to force effective action to give our Aborigines a fair deal.

Letters, Michael Sawtell. I am not generally in favour of bannings and prohibitions, but in this instance I think that it is wise for the Chief Secretary's Department to ban the Aboriginal film.

Aboriginal welfare has improved enormously in the last 20 years, but there are many people in Australia and overseas who have no idea what is being done to help our Aborigines to become assimilated. In fact, **it could be argued**, in some instances, that **we are now trying to do too much**.

The film could easily feed the persecution complex held by some of the mixed bloods. **This dwelling on the past is most destructive for both Aborigines and whites.** It can be seen among miners, many of whom are always harping about the time when women worked in mines.

Letters, Max Brown. From my own observation in south and north-western Australia, I would say that natives are frequently subjected to brutal treatment, and constantly subjected to stupid treatment – a condition that, by many accounts, is superior to the barbarism handed out in parts of the Territory and Queensland.

Behind the Aboriginal's primitive exterior lives stoic courage, respect for law, human warmth, and a passionate intelligence.

The sooner we realise this, the sooner will we face the inevitable necessity to improve policies and build a coloured race – already related by blood to us – of whom we can go proud and unashamed.

At the moment we are "ashamed," and the action of the Chief Secretary's Department and Commonwealth

Film Censorship points that fact nakedly to the 500 million marching coloured folk of the world.

Comment. We all know that changes have gradually occurred, but still have a long way to go. Later in this 1950's decade, many people started to agitate, each in their own way. Gradually, these agitators came together and did some good work raising public awareness of what a rotten deal the Aborigines were getting.

Then in the late 1960's, various Governments introduced a number of laws that helped quite a bit, but still by 1970 there was quite a back-log of citizens that clung to their old prejudices against our blacks.

PETER DAWSON SINGS SYDNEY'S PRAISES

Peter Dawson was a great local baritone singer who entertained for decades in Australia and overseas. He was famous for his War-time song "On the Road to Mandalay." He was now ending his career at the age of 71, and was spending his hobby-time fighting Tax Departments around the world.

He was originally from Adelaide, but had spent much time in Sydney. Never particularly reticent, he was quite happy to give Sydney the following reference.

"Sydney is the Paris of Australia – all froth and bubble – and I'm damned if I like froth and bubble. It's a terrible place. They have the hardest pavements anywhere and their tram lines stick up three feet out of the ground.

"And the trams – my goodness, you have to be an acrobat to get on them. Do you know there are some elderly people who haven't been into the city for years because they aren't game to get on the trams? Now they've put the taxi fares up to force more people onto them. Buses are just as bad. What used to be a 2d ride is 14d now.

"I always get a feeling in Sydney that I'm hemmed in. The streets are too narrow and the buildings seem about to crash down on you.

"They should move Randwick, the Showgrounds, and the abattoirs right out into the bush – miles away where there is plenty of space – and move the township in."

NEWS AND TRIVIA

News item. Here's some really good news for you. The militarists in the world, ever-working to make the world a safer place, reached an important milestone on May 27. The US announced that the world's first atomic shell was fired that day in the desert at Nevada. It was fired from an atomic cannon soon after dawn. Nine men loaded the 44 foot shell into the cannon, and it was fired from a control tower 10 miles away, after the gun crew had cleared the area. The shell was fused to explode at 500 feet above the ground at a distance of eight miles from the gun. Specimen targets had been set up. These included 50 trees, a 45-foot locomotive, 15 railway carriages, trucks, tanks, planes and guns. Rabbits, mice, and pigs and were in pens inside the target area.

Two pilotless F80 jets flew two monkeys and 30 mice through the atomic cloud. Sabre jets were on standby ready to shoot down the F80s if they behaved erratically and threatened nearby civilians.

Press Release, May 11. Thirty members of the Australian Contingent (to the Coronation) who attended the Australia-Surrey cricket match on Saturday at the Oval were under orders not to barrack. When they paraded at Purbright to collect their tickets, an officer gave them some advice on behaviour at an English match.

He said that the manners of the crowd at the Sydney Cricket Ground differed very much from that at The Oval, and that barracking would not be tolerated. He emphasised that "Have a go" would not be appreciated. If the words "ya mug" were added, the effect would be devastating.

Letters, Ellen Kent Hughes. The high price of milk is a cause of great concern to those who have to care for children.

Every child under 14 years of age needs 1½ pints of fresh milk daily, and thus a family consisting of two adults and four children needs at least four quarts of milk daily. The cost of this is approximately 10 Pounds a month, which is beyond the means of most wage-earners.

Separated or skim milk contains all the nutrient properties of whole milk, except the fats, and especially in hot weather is more easily digested. If arrangements were made by which this valuable food could be sold and distributed at a reasonable price, it would be a great boon to mothers.

Years ago, I practised in a district in Queensland, where there was a butter factory. The milk was very rich and upset many babies in the summer. I arranged for a special can of separated milk to be delivered to the homes of these children, and they thrived on it.

Letters, Social Worker. The article referring to the **preference for girls shown by adopting parents** interested me, but I wonder whether your correspondent had delved deeply enough.

Curly hair, blue eyes, pretty dresses, etc., are surely the superficial considerations. It would imply that adoption was intended to satisfy a whim of the female partner, but is not the husband equally concerned in the decision?

The husband is accepting this child as his son or his daughter. Such acceptance involves not merely an object for his affections, but an extension of his self carrying on his name, inheriting his property. "Will this child I adopt turn out to be worthy of ME" is a natural question for a prospective adopting father to ask himself. If there is any feeling of reservation, it is safer to adopt a girl who will marry and take another name; but a boy retains the family name and hands it down. Thus is the adopting father concerned in the selection of the sex of the child to be adopted.

Comment. The journalist who wrote the original article explained that some of the children were up to four years old. They had developed their personalities, and most of the boys were already belligerent and not prepared to accept discipline. This of course meant that prospective parents were reluctant to take a chance on a boy.

JUNE: QUEEN ELIZABETH

By the First of June, Princess Elizabeth had only a couple of days left to change her mind. Most people in Oz had already decided that she would go ahead, and were starting to live it up. Thousands of school children were finishing the rehearsals for pageants round the nation, shoppers in the major cities were pouring into the shops to buy souvenirs for the grand event, and half a million families jammed into the city centres to look at the street and city-store decorations. It was, we were told by ecstatic shopkeepers, much worse than Christmas.

To add to the thrill, Civil Honours were announced for worthy Australians. Prominent politicians, Harold Holt and Jack McEwan, both Members of the Government of the day, were appointed as Privy Councillors. Eleven more knighthoods were given, for notables like Garfield Barwick, later Govenor General of Oz, runner Marjorie Jackson, Joan Hammond as a singer, and Hudson Fyshe, as the effective founder of Qantas. In Britain, among the distinguished recipients were English cricketing opening-batsman Jack Hobbs, and the renowned jockey, Gordon Richards, both household names in Australia.

In England, as you would expect, things were almost frantic. Soldiers and Guards, horses and plumes, Bobbies and crowds of millions, Royals and their families, palaces and cathedrals, and garden parties and Poets Laureate were all jumbled together in mad excitement. Then ultimately, along came the Queen, with her usual majesty, and completely stole the show with her sincerity, poise, and a calmness that belied the whirling masses, and once again stole the hearts of died-in-the-wool patriots such as me. Prince Phillip also turned up, and was suitably attendant on her. Charles and Anne were visible a little later back at the Palace as they all came out and waved to the vast crowds.

The whole thing was a magnificent ceremony, carried out with the mastery and planning that the British always muster, and it cemented the Royal Family and monarchy firmly in place in Britain and the Empire for decades to come.

Here in Australia, huge crowds turned out to listen to the Coronation on the radio in public places, and many of them went to Church at the time of the ceremony, or to somewhat later services. Pageants were held in all major cities, people relished the public holiday that had been called, and even the most hardened cynics – of which there were few – had to remember the nobility of Elizabeth's late father, and her worthiness for the role.

The British-based Churches were warm in their appreciation. **Major-General the Rev C A Osborne** said at a special pre-Coronation service at St Andrew's Cathedral yesterday morning that of all the Queen's Dominions, Australia had perhaps the greatest need for vision and leadership.

"You remember the phrase in the Queen's Christmas broadcast when she spoke of keeping alive the courageous spirit of adventure," he said.

"That is the spirit for the new Elizabethan era that is dawning. It is the time for extending the Christian spirit.

"The Queen has asked us to pray for her, and we ask God to bless our young Queen, who will dedicate herself anew to the service and welfare of the people of the British Commonwealth of Nations.

"The coronation is something more than a pageant, and if we are to help the Queen at this the greatest moment of her destiny, let us rise to spiritual heights and let us dedicate ourselves to the service of God and the Queen."

The Rev D J Flockhart said at St John's Church, Wahroonga, yesterday that Queen Elizabeth came to the Throne steeped in tradition. The British people were proud of their Queen and her queenly qualities.

"We see in her the promise, even the embodiment, of the virtues which British people esteem, such as love of the home and family, devotion to justice and service, pity for the poor victims of misfortune and tyranny, and above all trust in God," he said.

Priests at the Catholics' Saint Mary's ignored the event, and gave rousing sermons on the importance of the battles, with the Turks, for Constantinople, in 1452.

CORONATION GRUMBLES AND WISHES

It seems that satisfaction levels were quite high about the entire ceremony. But inevitably, not everyone back home in Oz was fully satisfied. A few people thought that things could be done better. Letters were prolific. Some of them were sensible.

Letters, A C Ward. Now that we have prayed, sung, shouted, and turned night into day with illuminations, could we citizens of Australia not bravely set a seal of realism on it all by declaring a "truce of God" in our **industrial relationships**?

I am aware that such a suggestion will meet with a mixed reception, mostly hostile. Yet it savours of hypocrisy to invoke heaven's blessing on our Queen if we vitiate that blessing by our malignant disunity.

No gift would please her Majesty more than a pacified Australia bent on fulfilling a worthy destiny.

Letters, D M R Robinson. Sydney's fireworks display on Coronation night was disappointing, as it was too long and too scattered.

I think it would have been much more effective if the same quantity of rockets and mortar shells could have been expended in say a quarter of an hour instead of an hour.

Letters, Pyrolatist. Many viewers must have been as disappointed as I was by the poor display of fireworks on Coronation night. Large spending on shows cannot be condoned unless they are properly organised.

How beautiful and impressive a really well-produced fireworks display can be was demonstrated on the Thames, opposite Westminster, on VE night, when, with the water softly illuminated by many coloured jets, a magnificent eruption of rockets culminated in a gigantic patriotic set-piece. The whole effect was enhanced by the use of appropriate background music, Handel's Water Music and Fireworks Suite, the Pomp and Circumstance March, "Merrie England," etc.

On future occasions our displays should be concentrated at one point, not scattered all over the harbour. Suitable music should be played and a set-piece ordered well in advance to round off the evening.

Comment. It is hard to argue with a pyrolatist.

Letters, R S Partridge. Who was responsible for the issue to Australian school-children of the cheap, flimsy booklet, so-called a Coronation memento? How long are they supposed to last, and how many children in years to come will still have them as souvenirs of this glorious occasion?

Surely, when many thousands of pounds have been spent on first-class return trips to London for our Parliamentarians and families, to be present at the Coronation festivities, a gift from the Commonwealth to the children could have taken a more permanent form.

Letters, Mother. I am the mother of one of the very disappointed children whose name was not drawn "out of the hat" to attend the Coronation display at the Cricket Ground. My other two children were among the chosen few.

I am writing to protest against this very unfair celebration for some children only. Why could it not have been held on two or three days, so that all children might have seen it, as I am sure our very gracious Queen would have wished?

These disappointments are hard enough to take in adulthood, but what child could accept such decision without feeling slightly embittered.

Letters, A Matthews. In Sydney this week every Coronation film one sees advertised is referred to as the "only official coverage" or just the "only" coverage, or the "only full length coverage," "the only colour film," etc..

Cannot, at least on this occasion, truth reign? Let us be told directly and fairly which are the newsreels, which are the short subjects, and which are the full-length films. Some of us may prefer to see the shorter pictures, while, no doubt, many want to see the complete Coronation films. The advertising of these films has become such a battle of confusion that poor Mr Public is in a state of confusion.

MAN REALLY AT THE TOP

The Coronation was not the only good news that thrilled the British Empire on that day. For the last month, a British expedition of climbers had been working their way, via a new back passage, to the peak of Mount Everest. Over the last week, they had come within striking distance of the top, but had been sent to their tents by a howling six-day blizzard. But then, two climbers went forth, and ultimately mounted the great peak. One of these was a 34-year-old New Zealander, **Edmund Hillary**. The other was **his Sherpa guide, Tensing Norgay**, aged 39, who was a veteran of many Everest attempts.

The news of the conquest was taken by runner to the expedition's base camp on Khumbu Glacier, to the radio post at Namche Bazdar, and from there to the British Embassy in Kathmandu (Nepal) so that it could be sent by Diplomatic channels to London to allow the Queen to exult in the announcement a few hours before the ceremony.

It is understood that the successful pair of climbers, at Stage Nine, just before they managed the final climb, were so certain of success that they rewarded themselves with a little party of cake and oxygen before pressing on.

Throughout the world, people of all races rejoiced and marvelled at the victory over the dark forces of the weather. However, the Sherpas en route were more dubious. They were worried that there might now be no more expeditions, and that their livelihood as guides would suffer.

Some others were uneasy lest the gods they believed to inhabit Everest's peak should be angry at the expedition's encroachment on the peak, and that disaster would come to the surrounding villages. They believed that had happened in 1934 when an expedition got fairly close.

In any case, the venture was a triumph for the Brits who organised the Party, and it also was claimed as a major triumph for the Empire throughout the Coronation. And, incidentally, for the next 60 years.

The leader of the climbing team, Colonel Hunt, and Hillary were each granted knighthoods a few days later. The London newspaper, the *Daily Herald*, suggested that Everest's name might be changed to Mt Elizabeth. It said, "No race has a better claim to write into the history books a wonderful success story. All the Western World which has watched with sympathetic admiration both the Coronation and Colonel Hunt's expedition would surely applaud such a change." As it turned out, there were quite a few spoil-sports **from outside the British Empire** who were not so keen on the idea, and it got no further.

KEEP YOUR HAIR ON

Over the last year in NSW, very gradually, the number of people who died from eating rat poison had slowly increased, and in fact, thirteen people had died a painful death from this cause. None of them had volunteered for this, and they had all had the poison administered over a period of weeks in their food. The fatal ingredient was thallium which could go undetected for a month or so, until it took its painful final toll.

In most cases, the wife of the family sought to gain her freedom by poisoning her husband. A couple of women had killed their husbands about five years ago, and had now returned for a second dip.

The only obvious symptom was that the hair of the victims started to fall out, and this slowly increased as the level of poison, retained in the body, rose. Early this month the public sat up and took notice because of a couple of recent deaths, and two men attempting separate suicides, using thallium. There was much wild talk at the time about banning the sale of this poison, though wiser heads prevailed.

Letters, R M Duncan, Pest Exterminator. Surely it must now be admitted that rat poison prepared from thallium is not a deadly poison, after having the evidence of the number of people who are still alive and well after having drunk rat destroyer prepared from thallium.

Milk is the great antidote, and I know of an instance of a cat being given a bottle of thallium poison in a dish of milk and it did not suffer the slightest ill-effects. Every bottle of thallium sold has the antidote endorsed on it.

It takes 25 milligrams of thallium to kill a kilogram weight of rat, whereas the only result from giving a child 125 milligrams of thallium would be to make its hair fall out without any ill effects to the child, and the hair would grow in again shortly.

There is no other raticide in the world equal to thallium, and the benefits derived from its use far exceed the disadvantages that someone may be able to murder another person or commit suicide by taking it. Let the Government consider the danger of a rat or mice plague before in any way restricting the use of thallium, which in 25 years has been responsible for no more than 10 deaths. Motor vehicles are responsible for more deaths in a week.

Comment. It is probably true that death through poisoning is not as common now in 2012 as it was 60 years ago.

Women are much more clinical about it, and now use guns and knives. Which is a bit of a disappointment to me, because back in that distant past there were **many thrilling radio serials** based on the wife-poisoning-the-husband theme, and the various counter plots that the awakened husbands dreamt up.

NOSTALGIA - SOMETHING TO CHEW ON

There were many men who walked around in 1953 with something in their pockets. First and foremost, every one carried a handkerchief. You could use these to blow your nose on, to stem the flow of blood, to wipe hamburger juice off your shirt, and to wipe away a lady's tears. None of the modern-day substitutes, like paper tissues, are at all useful for such niceties, so most of these activities have doubtless ceased.

Then there was the fob pocket. This little sac was at the top of the trousers on the right-hand side. Into this, men could put their loose change. It would take about three pennies and a few threepenny and sixpenny coins and half a dozen shillings and florins. Given that many purchases needed a supply of small coins, this was a much-used treasure chest.

The well-dressed gentleman also had a fob pocket in his waistcoat. In this, resting on his right bottom rib, he had a gold watch with a chain attached, and this ran across his belly to a stud on his left bottom rib. These wonderfuly pretentious combinations were dying out, but the nobs in the capital cities still wore them on formal occasions.

Left-side and right-side pockets were in trousers, and every coat had three pockets. The top one was small and useless, but the other two carried all sorts of necessary stuff.

No real man would think of going out into the world without at least one packet of chewing gum in his coat pocket. Doubtless all readers will remember these Wrigley's products. Each packet contained four units, each about one inch long, coated in white sugar, and having strong flavour that lasted a minute before you got down to the gum.

There were *PK, Spearmint, and Juicy Fruit* flavours. You might chew on them for 15 minutes and after that they grew stale, so you stuck them on the bottoms of chairs or in the hair of someone else's dog. If you had to stop chewing, for some reason, you normally stuck them behind your ear and started again after the nuisance had gone. They were a bit stiff at this stage, but you could work them up.

From 1950, in Australia, you could supplement these Wrigley's products with bubble gum. With this, a small pink bubble would come out of the mouth, and slowly grow, then burst after it reached a six-inch diameter. At that stage, you sucked it back into your mouth, chewed it a dozen times, and blew another bubble. This was a clever tool for a girl with a pretty face when an unwanted suitor wanted a kiss. After the bursting, the said suitor rarely came back for more.

I might mention that trousers had another feature that has gone away with time. They had cuffs. And they had wide legs. I really enjoy now watching Boomers and their children getting out of their jeans and skin-tight pants.

For some reason they think they look good, but I know that my old-style broad legs with cuffs make me look much better. But in any case, I can get them on and off without surgery.

JULY: DOING IT TOUGH IN PRISON

When criminals in NSW were sentenced to prison, there was quite a variety of gaols they could be sent to. Inevitably, some of the more intractable were seen as being particularly dangerous to society and to other prisoners, and so were sent off to tough venues. One particular prison that stood out was at Grafton, 400 miles up the coast from Sydney, and its reputation for uncompromising discipline was legendary.

In early July, half a dozen convicts escaped from there. They included the notorious Darcy Dugan, who had been convicted for murder, and who had previously led the police a merry dance before being brought to justice. The escapees from Grafton were re-captured and, as you will pick up from the Letters below, were given harsh treatment. This raised the question of whether such measures were in any way justified, and whether they served any useful purpose.

Letters, Oscar N Trebitsch. The sentences imposed on Darcy Dugan and other convicts for their attempted escape from Grafton Gaol should, in a cultured community, not pass unheeded.

Many highly civilised countries make wide allowance for the **innate urge** in every imprisoned being to regain freedom, and therefore **do not consider an attempt to escape as a legal offence in itself**.

It must be bluntly said that the punishments ordered at Grafton (four weeks on bread and water followed by six months' of solitary confinement) lack completely the only morally acceptable justification of punishment, which is the ethical improvement of the criminal and the protection of the community from a repetition of the crime. To achieve this you must not half starve your fellow-man systematically, and drive him into utmost desperation. To do so means nothing but revengeful torture, very akin to the mentality of the evil old convict times and Pinchgut traditions.

England, well known to all criminologists for not pampering her criminals, does not enforce a water-and-bread diet for longer than 15 days, and after three days of this diet the convict must receive ordinary rations for the same time.

Must we so "colonial" and cruel as this?

Letters, E C Hartley. I wish to support Dr Trebitsch's moving indictment of the barbarous punishments imposed on prisoners in NSW and elsewhere or breaches of prison discipline.

Bread and water punishment, which means the semi-starvation of a prisoner for 28 days except for 1lb of bread daily, and solitary confinement in cells and cages on a punishment diet for a further 186 days, are harmful physically and mentally. Surely they must wreck the spirit of the individual and render him more desperate and anti-social than before.

Letters, N Mann. The Grafton punishments seem to be in the nature of vengeance. Discipline should be established by exactness and tuition, not by starvation and solitude. The greater the penalty, the harder the individual may become. It behoves the Department to help and not to destroy the small goodness that may be left in a convict's character.

Letters, E Hannan. It is not a punishment to impose solitary confinement and starvation. It is revenge and is barbarous and inhuman.

This can never reform. The prisoner's thoughts in his cage must be of hate for mankind, never reformation.

Letters, E E V Collocott. As a visiting gaol chaplain I saw much kindly interest being taken in prisoners by officials, but there were occasions when the scales seemed weighed against the prisoner.

So much of the discipline is humiliating and useless, tending to make a man worse than he was before. To take a man and condemn him to sit idle and alone, in a small and dreary space, for practically the whole of the 24 hours, day after day; to reduce eating and drinking to the most monotonous levels able to sustain life – these methods are unimaginative and cruel.

In the last analysis, men are in prison because, for one reason or another, their lives have been without normal creative interests. Deliberately to reduce their lives to the level of greatest possible monotony seems a sure way to increase the hopelessness that makes men anti-social.

We should not criticise prison officials for the way they do their job with the means given them. But as a community we should encourage and support those who are bringing fresh, more scientific, attitudes and methods to the treatment of society's sicknesses.

Letters, Shellback. Sixty years ago the law here in Australia sentenced me to 14 days' imprisonment for desertion of my ship.

Fourteen days' solitary confinement on a daily ration of six ounces of bread and a bucket of water. It seemed more like six months. **But it did not make me an enemy of society.** It was, indeed, a useful corrective that served me well.

Today far too much sympathy is extended to the gunman, the "basher," and the other criminals who seem to think it is right to prey upon society. The gaols of Australia hold far too many of them – young men for whom there is no excuse for a life of crime.

Men today who are in their 20s have not been affected by the War. Since it ended there has been honest work for every one of them, at high rates of pay – yet they choose crime. What they lack is discipline, and in gaol they ought to get it.

Considerable numbers of the inhabitants of our gaols have spent much of their time handing out cruel punishment to their fellow creatures. They are "toughs" – and a tough should be able to stand the rub of punishment when it comes to him, for a change. **Pity for him is misplaced.**

Comment. At the present time, in 2016, the problem remains just as it was 60-odd years ago. Prison authorities are still faced with prisoners who want to escape, and they can scarcely let that go unpunished. But what level of punishment can be used? Reformers say go easy on them, gaolors-on-the-job say you must be tough. The pendulum swings back and forth, but it seems that the only thing that changes is where to draw the line, rather than any material change in philosophy – to a new approach that I admit I have no concept of.

ANOTHER DOSE OF THALLIUM

The thallium epidemic among housewives showed no sign of abating, and indeed it hit a high point with the arrest in early July of a woman, for the unlawful use of the poison. The woman, Mrs Caroline Grills, was already on remand for having administered poison, with intent to murder, to two women. Then, on July 8th, she was separately charged with the murder of four other persons, and the attempted murder of another man. The victims were related to Mrs Grills by marriage, and three of the dead were women. One of the bodies had been exhumed, two had been cremated, and the other was recent and had not been buried. Mrs Grills was remanded in custody.

Over the next few weeks, various public figures made a series of silly suggestions that were taken seriously by a few people. For example, they suggested that thallium compounds should be now sold only under licence through chemists. The loud response was that it was mainly farmers with a rat problem that bought the product, and the prospect of applying for a licence and then going to a chemist was out of the question. Then there was a suggestion that imports of the products should be restricted. This gained favour in a few quarters until it was pointed out that the imports were only one per cent of the current market, so there would be no point in stopping these.

So, nothing was done.

The *SMH* did not like this inaction. The Minister for Health for NSW, Mr Sullivan, had been unwise enough to down-play the epidemic and say that the publicity was silly and a lot of rubbish. He said that newspapers were encouraging the illicit use of thallium, and they should refrain from mentioning it. The *Herald's* Editorial response was that thallium can be bought as easily as a bottle of cough mixture, and because it was colourless and tasteless, it was easy to administer. It went on to say that there had been 50 cases of poisoning in the last year in NSW and more than a dozen had been fatal. All other States had imposed at least some other restrictions on its distribution. Finally, it asked why have Mr Sullivan and his advisors been so slow to act? Could the State afford to wait while they pursued their leisurely investigations?

Mr Sullivan might have been rueing the publicity being given, but then it got out of hand. Bobby Lulham was a First Grade Rugby League player. He had recently represented Australia in a Test Series against Britain, and was regarded as one of the finest wingers in the game. As such, he was seen as a sporting hero by thousands of League followers.

On Saturday, July 21st, he played a Grade game and in it he missed a number of opportunities he would have taken readily under normal circumstances. He felt slow, sick, and disoriented. By Monday, his situation had deteriorated and he was admitted to hospital. A phone call from an unknown woman alerted the attending doctor to the fact that it would be worth checking him for thallium poisoning, and such was found to be the cause. For a few days he was seriously ill, but never critical, and his later recovery was complete.

This news released a flood of publicity about the dangers of thallium. There was no way that the Press could refrain from mentioning it, and in fact, it turned into a media frenzy. The evening Papers in particular enjoyed it all very much, and their lurid suppositions as to the identity of the villain were many and varied. But as it turned out, as usual, the perpetrator was close to home, and was a woman of his household. A Mrs Monty, his mother-in-law had been having an affair with Lulham and was charged as the perpetrator, and found guilty.

In the face of all the publicity that the matter received, the State Government was prompted to stir itself, and over the next few months, it brought down restrictions on the use of the product. A few other women were found guilty about the same time, and most of them were given prison terms, but the battered woman syndrome was often cited, and in a few cases, the penalties were very light indeed.

Bobby Lulham was unfairly subjected to on-field comments by a few football followers, and abandoned his career in Rugby League.

MIND YOUR LANGUAGE

The United Nations, after its inception, had given Australia a mandate to look after large areas of Papua and New Guinea. Of course, this was a region that was very primitive by Western standards, and the people varied from head-hunters in some mountain regions, to the better-educated folk of Port Moresby. But no one could say the society there was at all sophisticated. In a very general way, it was part of Australia's task to bring Western influences to bear on the population to make conditions there better than they had been in the past.

This involved the education of the people, at all levels. To help do this, pidgin English had the advantage that it was reasonably well established and provided some means of communication. On the other hand, it was a primative, restricted language with little scope for any form of sophistication.

Every year or so, the United Nations would send a Mission party of worthy delegates to visit New Guinea and pronounce on how well Oz was managing its mandate. In 1953, as usual, its advice on various matters was quietly ignored. But its comments on pidgin were picked up and gave rise to the following Letters.

Letters, D Clifton-Bassett. In his article of July 18, Sidney Baker says that the demand of members of the UN Visiting Mission to New Guinea that Australia should drop the use of pidgin English among the native of New Guinea would evoke from the knowledgeable philologian "a rather rough sort of laugh."

I agree with Mr Baker that expediency is the major factor determining its use; but I think that expediency requires that the domination of pidgin be ended as soon as possible. The futility of pidgin English is seen when we imagine a native trying to study, discuss, or instruct by medium of pidgin English, subjects such as economics, medicine, agriculture, politics, ordinary business transactions, or any of the arts and sciences.

Pidgin can be regarded as a full, mature language only if we expect the natives to settle down to their present level of culture. The only reason why there are pidgin English newspapers and radio broadcasts is that there are no other means of communication with the masses. The Department of Education has made English a compulsory subject in all schools since the War, and there is no reason to conclude that English will not replace pidgin English within a few generations.

The most important factor of all is the fact that the natives themselves realise their limitations by being restricted to pidgin and crave instruction in English. They are coming to regard pidgin as a badge of caste, and resent it.

Letters, Colin Simpson. In pidgin English, in order to say "I write" I should have to say, "Mi putim mark long pepa."

Convoluted as the worst "officialise," so crude that there are certain words in its vocabulary that you would not publish on the grounds of obscenity, Melanesian pidgin is a lingo so limited and ludicrous that one can well understand the UN Trusteeship Council calling on Australia to put an end to its use in New Guinea.

What is disturbing is, from my own observations in New Guinea, that there is no real will to replace pidgin with English, and that there is still, among a section of the Europeans there, what the American sociologist Reed in his book "The Making of Modern New Guinea" noted as "a definite hostility towards the native being given any education at all."

James L Taylor, described pidgin to me bluntly as a dead-end language and a slave language, and said that any move to end pidgin is "unreal."

Pidgin is useful, expedient, a necessary first-step makeshift means of communication and has been of great value. But it cannot get the natives anywhere. Our native education record in New Guinea is nothing of which Australia can be very proud. Most of the education process is left to the missions. Kwato Mission, in Papua, has always taught its natives English, with the result that they are the most "advanced" in the joint Territory, but many of the other missions give a sub-standard teaching which, though heavily subsidised, is most inadequately supervised.

There is no future for the native in a "language" that calls on him to express the number eleven as "wanpela ten wan." Pidgin is a caste tongue, a lingo for lesser-breeds, inferiority made half-articulate. The rate at which it is being replaced with English among the 1,000,000 people of New Guinea is so slow at present that one is forced to the conclusion that the Trusteeship Council's prodding of Australia to do better, faster, is fully justified.

Comment. There might have been some measure of agreement among the above writers, and indeed through the entire white population of New Guinea. But reform was hard to put into practice, and the UN Missions a decade later still made comments about how little progress had been made in this matter.

NEWS AND VIEWS

Letters, Arline Lower, New Australian Culture Association. As an Australian-born citizen who enjoys the confidence and friendship of a great number of newcomers, I should like to give some reasons why the **various national groups should be permitted to lay a wreath on the Cenotaph on the days of their national mourning.**

Having become naturalised Australians, or having signified their intention of doing so when the required five years have elapsed, they feel that by laying a wreath on the Cenotaph in memory of their loved ones who have perished in the cause of freedom, they are identifying themselves with Australia's national life, and, at the same time, sharing in a very real manner the sacred traditions of their new homeland.

Moreover, many of our New Australians fought side by side with Australian-born soldiers. There is in Sydney a Polish "Rats of Tobruk" Association. Last November many national groups worked gladly for months to prepare for the "All Nations Fair," the proceeds of which were used for the welfare of the children of the men to whose memory the Cenotaph was erected.

We should remember that it is not merely in finding work and supplying homes for our new settlers that true assimilation takes place. It is in sharing with them the spiritual life and the common destiny of our nation that this will be accomplished.

AUGUST: HILLARY ON HIS VICTORY LAP

The newly knighted Edmund Hillary came to Sydney town early in August. At a reception at the Town Hall, the *SMH* described him as a fluent, graceful and humorous speaker. He never hesitated in choosing a word, and he did not waste words. It had been reported earlier that he was a shy taciturn man, awkward in society, and only happy when at high altitudes or in silent communication with his bees. Such reports were wrong.

After the reception, he handled his interview in a relaxed manner while he had one sherry.

An interviewer said solemnly: "When you reached the summit, didn't you feel detached from the world – up there in that icyness?"

"We were detached from the world, I suppose," said Sir Edmund. "But that didn't stop us from being damn keen to get down again. We didn't want to stay up there."

"Is it true that you were awarded an Order by the Government of Nepal?"

"Yes, a very big Order. It comes right across here." Sir Edmund showed how far it spread across his chest. "The Kathmandu taxi-drivers gave me a medal, too."

"Does that mean you'll get free taxi rides in Auckland?"

"No. And I won't get free taxi rides in Katmandu, either."

"Was Tensing upset about that silly controversy over who got to the top first?"

"Yes, he was very distressed. We thought we had just been climbing a mountain. But we found we had got into a political conflict with no holds barred."

PEACE IN KOREA AT LAST

At long last, the militarists and diplomats in Korea, on both sides, had come to the obvious conclusion that there was no further propaganda value to the war there, and they might as well pack up and go home. It turned out such a change in attitude was made possible by **two big political events** at home. **Firstly**, in the US, President Harry Truman ended his term of office, and he was succeeded by Eisenhower. This newcomer could see no reason why his administration should be saddled with the expense and hassle of a war that was going nowhere, and he was happy to move his Generals round and introduce a deliberate quest for peace.

Secondly, in Russia, Communist leader Joe Stalin died, and his death precipitated many uncertain moves at the top. But, once again, peace was no longer a dirty word. So both sides pulled out all stops, and an armistice was signed on the 8th of August.

Comment. This was not a full settlement of all issues. It only stopped the fighting. It meant that the Armed Services could pick up sticks and make their way back towards home. It meant that bombings of military and civilians would stop. And it meant that POWs would all be released. It was indeed a big step forward.

But there was still plenty to be done. Remember, jumping ahead a little, that Korea was ultimately divided into two parts, along the 38th Parallel with a very wide de-militarised zone that kept, and still keeps, the populations separated from each other. And remember that the hostility between the two halves is still officially as great as during the war. The Armistice stopped the war but, sixty years later, it has not stopped the propaganda war and the childish posturings on both sides of the border.

Second Comment. Once again, it was most noticeable just how little enthusiasm there was in Australia for this war. You might have thought that after three years, Australia would have made a big thing of the armistice and that, for example, the Papers would have been full of it. But this was not the case. The *Sydney Morning Herald* announced the signing of the cease-fire as the second lead-story of the day, in just two columns. As I explained more fully in the 1951 and 1952 books of this series, the entire War justly earned the title then, and now, of the "Forgotten War", because of the sheer folly of its inception, motivation and execution. Sadly too, the Australian men who fought it on our behalf have since become Forgotten Heroes.

Should the Churches celebrate the armistice? A few persons of prominence came out and said that our Churches should very explicitly celebrate the end of hostilities. This seemed to most people a natural and sensible thing to do. After all, we would now put an end to the killing of Australian troops, they would come home and, economically, the nation would stop spending vast monies on someone else's war.

Everyone realised that it was in fact just an armistice, an end to the fighting, and that there was a long way to go before the settlement of a full peace treaty would happen. But surely, they asked, could not the end of the fighting be celebrated in our Churches? As it turned out, **two prominent clergymen** thought it should not be.

Firstly, in Brisbane, Bishop Dixon described celebrations as untimely, and emphasised that "it was only a truce, a military thing, very easily broken." He advised the nation to wait for further developments. **Then in Sydney**, Reverend Woolcock decided that "all this excitement seems rather sickening" and the celebration suggestions were out of place, and seemed to be mistaking the functions of the Churches. "Anyone would think the war was over."

Rev Woolcock supported his sermon with the following.

Letters, (Rev) George Woolcock, Congregational Church. With reference to your leader in the "Herald" of August 4, my main concern is not with this truce in Korea, but with its aftermath.

What is to follow? I may be a "man of peace" but not peace at any price. When the whole intricate and complicated business of Korea has been satisfactorily settled, and "peace with justice" has been assured, and the tremendous sacrifices of our men have not been whittled away in political wrangling and top-level discussions, then I say by all means let us unfurl the flags and ring the bells and "go to town" with services of thanksgiving.

At present we are baptising the baby before it is born!

One Letter-writer saw it all very differently.

Letters, Paddie Flynn. If we accept that the amount of prayers we can proffer is limited, we should work out when is the best time to offer them. In the case of the Korean War, the best time would have been at the start. Then we could have prayed **the persons promoting** it would be wiped from the face of the earth before they killed **the millions of people that they ultimately killed**.

Surely God would have acted had he thought that they were planning to go fight their war in some country that no one had ever heard of, and divide an initially unified nation into two warring bits, bitterly hating each other. He surely would have acted if he had realised that dozens of nations would send troops to be killed in a fight that was just designed to bring glory to the two nations that were promoting it.

We don't need church services now for Korea. What we need is some sort of international Court that will take the persons responsible for the war, and find them guilty and punish them terribly. **That is what we should pray for now.**

The *SMH* was wise enough to stay clear of the last Letter. But it did comment on the views of the two clergy previously. It argued that of course no one knew what would happen to Korean peace in the future, but the simple fact that the guns had ceased firing was cause for us to be thankful. Surely, all clergymen, as men of peace should rejoice in the cessation of war. Would not the families of our active military over there be thankful? Would not the soldiers and airmen themselves who were facing death every minute of every day, be thankful?

Surely, *the Herald* said, those clergy who were opposed to the holding of services should reconsider their positions.

Letters, (Rev) A Allan Bennett. Although greatly disappointed at the apathy displayed by the general public to the suggestion of Sir Arthur Fadden that thanksgiving be made to Almighty God for the armistice in Korea, I do not share the views publicly expressed by the Rev C A Woolcock that thanksgiving is premature.

I am one who believes there should be more frequent thanksgivings for small blessings as well as large.

We knew that we were not thanking God for peace, but I suggested to my congregation that it was a cause for great thankfulness that the armistice had been agreed upon, and that the following were adequate reasons for calling people to thanksgiving and prayer:

One. It provides a most hopeful indication that the aggressors are beginning to realise that aggression will not succeed; **two,** it provides a most welcome respite from human slaughter with the preservation of precious life on both sides; **three,** it provides an opportunity for sick and weary prisoners to be restored to their homes.

We thanked God for all this, and also for the incentive to still more earnest prayer that in the forthcoming conference some basis may be found whereupon a permanent and abiding peace may be established.

Comment. I think the last word on this matter should go to the following Letter.

Letter, Tom Grahame. No matter what some clergy say, I am getting on my knees every night now and thanking God that my two sons in Korea are out of their trenches and will be home in a few weeks.

POMS GOING HOME

Since the War, there had been a steady stream of Britishers migrating to Australia, under a variety of schemes. Many of them had come with assisted passage, many had been guaranteed appropriate jobs, many had been promised accommodation for a few years, and only a few had come out independently of any government aid. By 1953, an alarming number of these migrants were turning round and going back, permanently severing their connections to Australia. This thoughtful Letter below sums up some of the matters involved.

Letters, G Bennett-Wood, UK Services and Ex-Services Association. The fact that 29,000 persons left Australia permanently in 1952 gives food for thought.

Those in close touch with the position must suspect that the number of British migrants who want to go back and can't afford the fare is very large indeed. In these circumstances it is surely time to ask why, exactly, so many of our kith and kin from the Old Country are anxious to go back home.

It is usual, of course, to label a British migrant who returns home as "disgruntled" and "a no-hoper anyway."

But it would be greatly to our interest, surely, to discover why they are "disgruntled" and why they have lost hope, and to seek some practical means of keeping them.

Comment. The above Letter stirred up a strong response from one Pom who had gone bach to England.

Letters, Margarette Smith. On March 24, 1952, I arrived in Australia as a prospective settler; and exactly one year later I booked my passage back to England. I will give some of my reasons.

First, taking the long view-point, I am a "no-hoper," because, unless all present economic and social tendencies are reversed, I can see no hope in the future of Australia as a white man's country. It is not the young, virile land of its own imagination – its arteries are prematurely hardening into the rigid caste of a bureaucratic, "welfare" State.

Australians themselves will not develop their own country – they are far too lazy. Sir William Slim has soon summed up the situation, and the theme of his speeches is already "produce and populate – or else!"

My guess is that the warning will go unheeded, and within a century Australia will have succumbed to Asiatic population pressure.

Secondly, from the personal angle, I can see no hope in Australia of ever finding the things that make life worth living for me, and I do not wish to adapt myself to what I imagine must be the lowest standard of living in the "westernised" world. A high standard of living to me does not mean a 12 Pound basic wage, steak three times a day, and a washing machine. Exactly what it does mean is difficult to put into words, but I know that it exists in War-battered Britain and Europe to a degree almost unimaginable here. It implies the availability of the ideas and products of a living culture based on foundations of long, historical tradition, expressed in such things as high standards of literature and book production, the theatre and concerts offering the classics of all ages by people of all countries, art galleries with their exchanging exhibitions, and a wide national Press catering for all levels of taste and interests; it means a Government and Public servants of whom one automatically expects integrity, and Public Services which one likewise expects to give service, and which produce surprise, not resignation, if they do not.

One of the most ludicrous things to an outsider is the constantly reiterated cry of the self-satisfied Australian that his products and activities are "of world standard" or equally often "the best in the world." The world to the majority of Australians is Australia, and they do not even know what goes on outside in order to make comparisons. I cannot face with equanimity a future in which I also must gradually slip behind and become isolated, in an apathetic, semi-fossilised condition.

Letters, Leonard A Blamey. My little family and I migrated from London to Sydney a year ago, and many times since I have had the inclination to turn and run. But I know I should not be very happy with myself for having done so.

The answer to Margarette Smith, is that this country is a challenge to our Western civilisation. Anyone can grow up and continue to exist in a civilised "cultured" State already prepared for them. Just sitting back in appreciation is certainly an easy, decadent form of living. If the civilisation and culture we believe in is really vital, then we shall desire fervently to see it expand and flourish, and strive to pass it on to the coming generations, even if they happen to be born in uncivilised Australia.

Margarette Smith, and maybe I, may feel unequal to the task ahead. We may turn and run, but even if we do, we can be sure that other people of greater courage will go forward with the task of creating a great continent. So how about it, Margarette Smith? Has not your culture given you something you would like to contribute and pass on?

Letters, Cameronia. G Bennett-Wood has asked a question of national interest. What made about 29,000 people leave this country last year for good?

Are they "disgruntled" or just "no-hopers"? Disgruntled, yes – but it could not be said they are "no-hopers" if they have saved their fares and are now prepared to start afresh in the Old Country.

Many a migrant has resigned a good position and come out here with a mental picture of security and progression. What disappoints him? The truth must be faced. The Australian is no authority on hospitality. The migrant finds him mercenary to the extreme, selfish, and absolutely lacking in gallantry and courtesy.

The case appears to be one of misrepresentation. The immigration contract is one-sided and it demands thorough investigation.

Out of a big number of migrants/settlers I have asked, "Would or will you, return to the Old Country?" the percentage answering in the negative was negligible.

For my own part, I know that I will have to return or be made a pauper in this country which promised me so much.

Letters, Housewife and Mother. I was most interested in the comments of Margarette Smith.

All she says is perfectly true: but there is a solution, and it lies with the women of Australia.

Please, women, come forward and stand for elections in local councils, State and Federal Governments.

I myself intend standing for the next election of our local council. Local councils invite co-operation. See your respective town clerks to-day. Council elections take place in December next.

I am finding support everywhere I go. The only person who is opposing me is my husband, and for this cause I am willing to risk divorce, jail, or death, so strongly do I believe in it.

Letters, Frederick Diggins. Margarette Smith says that it is ludicrous for the self-satisfied Australian to claim that his country's products are equal to, or even better than, world standard.

Has Miss Smith been to our Royal Agricultural Society's annual Easter Show in Sydney?

To claim that the livestock and produce at this exhibition are not of world standard would be ridiculous.

Letters, Pommy Migrant. An Englishman myself, I have read the comments of Margarette Smith. She does not tell us why English migrants go home.

The fact is that shortages, rationing, and housing problems in England (they are still short of three million homes) are so acute that since the War most married couples live with mother; and mother waits on them and rears their kids.

As soon as they "make a break" and migrate here, they have not the ability or courage to stick it out on their own. They want their mothers' help. Severe nostalgia sets in and they are not happy till they return.

I have to-day an English family with me; together they earn 30 Pounds a week. In England their combined wages were 7 Pounds. The woman is taking her husband home next month with her sons.

THE PRICE OF MILK BOTTLES

News Item. Sydney milk distributors face such big losses on lost milk bottles – which cost them more than 5½d each – that they may have to charge consumers a deposit of 6d for a pint bottle.

The chairman of the Milk Board, Mr J A Ferguson, said yesterday that the Board was considering allowing the charge to help solve the problem. He said the deposit would be refunded to customers when they returned the empty bottle, or the bottle could be exchanged for another full one.

Mr Ferguson said that there are at present about 10 million bottles in circulation in the Sydney metropolitan area. Their value is about 250,000 Pounds. The "life" of each bottle is about 25 to 30 trips.

Agents "are allowed to charge ½d a pint to replace bottles, clean and sterilise them after use, and fill and cap them."

Mr Ferguson said that about 45 per cent of the milk delivered in Sydney was now delivered in bottles. By December this would probably have increased to 60 per cent. The other current 55 per cent comes from dippers that the milkman carries to the house, and then pours it into jugs left out for this purpose. Generally, a fly-cover of a small net is placed over the top of the jug. Within two years it was hoped that all milk would be sold in bottles.

Mr Ferguson said that the Board had considered the use of pint cardboard containers to distribute milk, but these lasted only one delivery and cost about 2d each.

The president of the Housewives' Association, Mrs Hilda Jesson, said last night: "What the housewife wants is more back-door service and less irksome controls. Milk is dear enough already without the imposition of deposits on the bottles."

Comment. Those jugs with milk made wonderful targets for paper-men doing their deliveries. To hit a jug from 30 yards away, while travelling at 30 miles per hour, was something to brag about.

WHAT TO WEAR TO THE RACES?

News Item. Top-hats will be worn in the Members' Enclosure at Randwick racecourse in the new season which opens on August 1. They have not been worn there since the War began.

The Australian Jockey Club Committee has asked members to wear full morning dress at the major meetings. The first of these will be Derby Day and Metropolitan Day on October 3 and 5 respectively.

The Chairman of the AJC, Mr Alan Potter, said last night the Committee was influenced by the approach of the Royal visit next year, and by requests from members themselves. Mr Potter said: "We were asked about formal dress at the last annual meeting. We feel that any objection that existed in the War and immediate post-War years no longer remains. Therefore we will return to pre-War practice and ask members to wear formal dress."

Mr Potter said there could not be any question of compulsion. The matter would be left to members themselves. At the Melbourne Cup meeting last November members, with few exceptions, observed the VRC committee's request to wear formal dress. Interstate visitors, a majority of them members of the AJC, did so, too. All those invited to the Committee enclosure wore formal dress.

NEWS AND VIEWS

Letters, George C Ghys. May I support those who have made known their objection to the **violation of the day of rest and meditation** by way of noise?

The great teachers, Christ, Buddha, and others less known, certainly did not give notice of their meditation by means of noise, but retired to places of quietness.

Bell-clanging and tom-tomming revert to the jungle where, on occasions, savages seek to dispel evil spirits.

Letters, LONG SUFFERER. Nature, which has endowed the suburb in which I live with unsurpassable beauties, may also have endowed us with the crowing rooster and the barking dog. But when these are combined with the morning bells, the blaring wireless, and screaming children, all of which are controllable by man, a place of beauty can become a joyless waste for ever.

Letters, R Bailey. A current film programme in this town includes an advertisement for soup set to music from the "Mikado".

If effect cannot be given to perpetuating the copyright to these works of Art by Act of Parliament, as was mooted in England, an appeal should be made to advertising agencies to show respect for music for which thousands must have a deep respect.

Press release. The company involved indicated that it would not use the Mikado in future ads. It was unsure what its future policy was towards Gilbert and Sullivan, but it assured the public that it had high regard for their music, and any use of it would be tasteful.

A Note for marsupial mole lovers. Letters, Ray Harris. Mr W Ketts seems to have confused eyes with the vestiges of eyes.

What he thinks are tiny eyes in the marsupial mole are tiny non-functional, nerveless scales where the eyes used to be. It is, therefore, no misconception that moles' eyes have disappeared.

And because moles are totally blind, Mr Kett's assertion that they are extremely sensitive to light cannot be accepted, I am afraid.

They have an awareness to heat in the ordinary way, but the fiercest sunlight could produce no more optical reaction in two nerveless, vestigial scales than it could in two corns or bunions.

SEPTEMBER: MY, HOW THINGS CHANGE

Over the next few pages, I have included reminders of some of the many aspects of 1953 things that I have more or less forgotten about, and which "progress" has made obsolete or old hat.

Shopping hours. Now, in 2016, we are accustomed to big stores being open on Thursday or Friday nights, and Saturdays and Sundays. Smaller shops often stay open till midnight, and some are open 24 hours a day.

Back in 1953, this was not the case. Petrol stations would open generally from 8 in the morning to about 6 at night, and for a few hours on Saturdays, and mostly not at all on Sundays. Big city stores were in the midst of never-ending controversies about Friday night and Saturday morning shopping. Below is a Letter expressing a view well ahead of its times.

Letters, Douglas Taylor. In Los Angeles, there is a frock shop that opens at 11o'clock in the morning and shuts at four in the afternoon; reopens at nine in the evening and shuts at three in the morning.

These may seem odd hours but the shop makes a profit, which shows that it is doing a service to the public. It is near an aircraft factory and sells goods to the workers at the hours they prefer to buy. The shop assistants work the normal 40-hour week.

Surely the criterion of when a shop should be open must be based on the amount of public support that it gets. The shopkeeper knows whether he is making a profit or a loss. If he is making a loss, obviously he is not getting sufficient public support to warrant continuing the service. If he is making a profit, it is quite clear that he has public approval of his hours of doing business.

The public should not tolerate job control either from shopkeepers or shop assistants. The public should decide.

Helicopter services. News Report. No doubt the questions uppermost in the minds of those who attended yesterday's conference at Lithgow to discuss the possibilities of helicopter travel were those of safety and reliability – and the economics of operation.

Manufacturers in Britain and America are estimating the prices of commercial helicopters at from A90,000 Pounds for a 14-seater to A245,000 Pounds for a 36-seater.

Large initial costs, therefore, are involved, and ratepayers at Katoomba, Bathurst, Orange and other centres where aldermen have announced keen interest in helicopter services will want the facts to be examined carefully.

Major air carriers in Britain, Europe and America have no doubt about the future of the helicopter as a public transport. They believe that it is destined to play an important part in internal transport systems over distances up to 300 miles.

Do passengers like helicopter travel? The British finding is that there has been little air-sickness. Passengers comment favourably on the improved view and on the intimate nature of the flying because the pilot is always insight. Many complaints, however, have been received about vibration.

Adverts on trams. Letters, C Millan Ashton, Civic Pride Society, Sydney. The Minister for Transport is reported to have announced that the sides of e of Sydney trams are to carry advertising.

This is a regrettable move which cannot be justified even on the ground that it is done elsewhere. No responsible Minister would ever dream of authorising advertising on our large fleet of smart departmental cars, so why spoil the appearance of the public transport of Mr and Mrs Citizen?

Stage expletives. Letters, E J. I would like to raise objection to a trend in theatre language observable in recent productions and more particularly in the current show "South Pacific."

Certain words are repeatedly shouted across the footlights with apparent relish by one of the female members of the cast, much to the distaste, I am sure, of a large number of the ladies present and to the embarrassment of their menfolk.

No respectable person would use these words in conversation nor permit their use in front of his womenfolk; indeed I recall police intervention when a drunk chose to use these exact words in a public place.

THE REDEX OIL RELIABILITY CAR TRIAL

The month of September belongs to the Redex Trial. This was a car reliability trial, the first of its sort in Oz since the War. The idea was that 186 standard cars would set out from Sydney, drive over defined roads to various cities round the eastern half of the nation, according to a given timetable. The Trial would be competitive, and the car and team that stuck to the timetable best of all would be the winners.

The route took the cars up the east coast to Townsville, then across to Darwin, down to Alice Springs, and Adelaide, eastwards again to Melbourne and up to Sydney. This was a total of 6,500 miles. A certain number of hours would be allowed for each car to complete a leg, and if it booked in at the appropriate time, it would lose no points. The later it was, the more points it lost.

This was supposedly a reliability trial. Some officials said it would prove which standard car would stand up best to tough, but not impossible, Australian conditions over a fair test. Others said it might be more like the conditions that a country doctor in a desperate hurry for 6,500 miles would experience racing across dirt roads and tracks. In any case, it was meant to sort out the sheep from the goats.

In theory, there was to be no replacement of major car parts, though most teams always sent another team well ahead with a bucketful of spare parts. Then again, drivers were supposed to proceed at a sedate though demanding pace through the various legs, and thus arrive dead on time. In fact, most of the dare-devils drove like mad so as to get twenty miles from the finish, so that if they had a problem on the way, they would have the time to fix it and still make their deadlines. There were all sorts of devices and dodges possible, and every one of these was liberally practised.

Each car was sponsored by some major manufacturer or supplier of cars, parts, oils, petrol, brakes, and so on. There were generally teams of two alternating drivers to drive, and a navigator, and most all of these were experienced round the various circuits and racetracks. A high percentage of them might be described as, shall I say, "adventurers", though many people thought they were cowboys and hillbillies. Still, they were a terribly lively pack and their exploits thoroughly captured the imagination of all Australia for three weeks, and gave the media the feeding frenzy of the year. It exceeded that of the Coronation (in Australia).

I will pick up the account of the Trial at various points along the tortuous way.

The trip from Sydney to Brisbane started urbanely enough. Five cars were forced to withdraw, and many suffered delays through damage from potholes and flying stones. The first competitor arrived in Brisbane at 9.32am, right on time. From then, until 7.30 pm, a procession of cars arrived, mostly at the scheduled three-minute intervals. There were 300 onlookers there to greet the first car. Police at Ballina booked 15 cars for speeding as they passed through the town. Many cars reached Brisbane up to three hours early, and they waited well short of the check-in, and used the time to survey their vehicles and make repairs. All in all, the trial was off to a good start.

The next day, after the Rockhampton leg, the number of cars was down to 173. There were some tough luck stories.

News reports. Patience and Binks failed to take a bend at the approach to the Gin Gin creek and hurtled over a 20ft embankment. Their car landed upside down and was crushed. Rescuers had difficulty in getting the men from the wreck. They are now in hospital. Patience is in a serious condition suffering severe concussion. Binks was also admitted to hospital for observation. It was stated that the car was following a Jaguar and a big petrol wagon, when, blinded by dust, Patience missed a road cutting running down to a low-level bridge.

Larymore had a remarkable escape. His car hit a series of potholes in part of the road where bitumen gives way to gravel. The car rolled over twice. Wager's car collided head-on with another Ford driven by Maurice Dahl, a grazier's son, near Miriam Vale. Gail Craig, 3, who was in the car driven by Dahl, suffered cuts to the face. First aid was given by a grandmother, Mrs Winn Conway, who arrived 25 minutes late at the control point as a result.

Early competitors were at a disadvantage today because of the fog and it is significant that the crashes occurred among the first few hours. "Although we left 6 hours 24 minutes behind the leading car, the fog was still impenetrable in places and drivers were forced to reduce speed to 20 mph. Many cars broke down under the arduous conditions today and about 40 have now lost points. The roads were rough and the temperature high."

The 609-mile stretch to Mt Isa really sorted out the field. Here is one reporter's account.

One driver, **Gelignite Jack Murray**, driving a Plymouth, turned his car over twice. The second time he was taken to Mt Isa Hospital with slight head injuries. Murray, who was accompanied by Bill Murray, a non-relative, first turned over near Julia Creek when he hit a bullock in a creek-bed. With the help of local residents, the battered car was righted and they set off again.

Outside Cloncurry, on the Mt Isa road, the car hit a "jump up." This is a series of sloping "steps" in the road. On a steep hill they are unnoticeable until the driver hits them. According to eye-witnesses, Murray's car hit one at speed, completed a corkscrew in the air, and landed upside down for a second time in four hours. "When we were passing the car, the Murrays were sitting alongside it, Bill holding a pad over his wounded head. They told us they were all right and that help was coming. One hundred yards before their crash, a Holden had hit a bank, wrecking it. The car had a "Mickey Mouse" mascot painted on the bonnet, but the crew all escaped injury."

Through the bush track from Charters Towers last night there was one long series of broken down cars, their crews busy tinkering by torchlight under the bonnets. When dawn came, drivers still in the trial saw wrecks all along the route. A red Citroen was wrapped around a post near Julia Creek. Two miles further on a Holden was jammed in a cattle crossing which had bars removed. After Cloncurry a Morris Minor crew was seen trying to repair a broken differential. Other crews, abandoning crashed cars, were walking back to civilisation.

And so it continued. By the time the cars got to Alice Springs, the drivers were exhausted, after driving an average of 500 miles a day for a week over mainly dirt tracks. On top of that, most of them were sleeping rough, under the stars, because there was no hotel accommodation that could house 1,000 people in the cities visited. Even worse, they found, they had just completed the 907 miles from Darwin in one continuous drive, and this had been "the most boring day of my life." Only 42 cars had not lost points and about 50 cars had withdrawn. Still they went on, to Kingoonya, and now reporters were sending in their stories **via pedal radio**.

By the time they reached Adelaide, drivers felt they had it made. They were on the home stretch, more or less, but importantly they were back on sections of the road that were sealed. Though about 50 cars at Adelaide were now reported as "missing." The drug benzadrine was being widely used to keep drivers awake.

By Melbourne, only eight cars had not lost points. Finally, at Sydney, at the Showground, the various teams got a rousing and fitting reception after their 15 day travels, and were roundly cheered in by a crowd of 40,000.

Now it can be told: a granny's tale

Mrs Winn Conway, a grandmother, took part in the Trial, accompanied by her husband. She said last night that a guard at the Woomera rocket range fired five shots over the top of her car when she drove on the wrong road.

Mrs Conway was present at a dinner in Sydney tendered to competitors in the Redex trial. "We were on a bit of a bush track and passed a shed," she said.

"I thought it was a blacks' camp and did not take any notice of it. A few minutes later, some character in a leather jacket came out and started firing shots over us," she said.

Mrs Conway said that her most embarrassing moment was on her arrival in Sydney when a large woman clasped her to her bosom and kissed her effusively.

A representative of Larke Hoskins told Mrs Conway when she arrived that the company would give her a new Austin Sedan if she would turn over to them the Austin tourer she had made famous. She was told that she would also receive a gold watch, studded with diamonds and rubies. Mrs Conway said, "Isn't that nice. I have not had a watch in 20 years.

"We have had a wonderful time and have enjoyed every minute of it. I'd like to go around again right now. We have had no trouble at all with the car. All that has been done to it on the trip is the normal greasing and servicing. We have not even had to put any water in it."

Mrs Conway said that they had not even "touched a twig" on the trip. Reports that her car had broken down between Alice Springs and Kingoonya were wrong. "We made a picnic of it," she said. "But I couldn't have completed the course without the help of my navigator and co-driver."

She added that at she had always wanted to tour the outback but had been too frightened to try it. But with so many men doing the Trial, she knew she was safe. Also, she was not at any time worried about the time part of the trial.. Very often, when conditions were nice, they stopped and had a picnic, or just a walk round the bush.

LETTERS ABOUT REDEX

Letters, Motorist. The statement by the Minister for Transport, Mr C E Martin, that future motor reliability trials will not be permitted to cause road congestion, and "before another reliability trial takes place we shall take action to ensure it is conducted in different circumstances," suggest lack of appreciation of the tremendous public interest in the Redex trial.

Probable reasons for this interest are: (1) Most of us are motorists in one way or another; (2) a very large number of us would like to see those parts of Australia which are on the trial route; (3) the route covers nearly 6,500 miles. An extremely exacting test of car and driver; (4) and the trial is an Australian event.

That neither the transport authorities nor perhaps anyone else foresaw the extent of the interest in the event is not surprising, but the competition is not to be condemned on that account. The interest shown may indicate that motorists themselves could do more towards "opening up" Australia than will railways and air services – given reasonably good highways.

In any case, it does seem to me to be somewhat short-sighted to disapprove by implication the spontaneous interest of 200,000 people.

Letters, Safety First. An official of the Redex trial has assured me that safety has been closely considered, but since the trial began, several contestants have been booked for speeding through a large country town. Now in the "Herald," I read that contestants have driven at speeds of 100 mph, and also that "most drivers are desperately in need of sleep."

Two most important causes of road accidents are excessive speed and fatigue. These evils seem to be very evident in this test on the public roads. It will be interesting to study the future toll of the road if motorists generally are to be allowed to try to cover as much ground in as little time as the contestants seem to be doing.

Letters, Fiat Justitia. I have been surprised to read of the number of cars in the trial to which repairs – often of a major nature – have been made, and which are allowed to continue.

It has been emphasised that this is a reliability trial, not a speed test, but surely there can be nothing reliable about a car which cannot complete 6,500 miles running, no matter what the roads are like, without innumerable repairs being made en route.

It would be more appropriate to penalise, if not eliminate, these cars for their failure to complete the course without mechanical breakdowns, rather than for their failure to reach check points within a specified time.

Letters, A J Ritchie. I think it is a matter of urgency, before the trial finishes, that the engine numbers and any other identification marks, chassis numbers, etc., be published for the protection of the public, who may later unwittingly buy one of these vehicles at an auction or private sale. One can imagine a deceptively simple ad: "Car for Sale, only done 6,500 miles, one owner." He might even put "one careful owner" if he gets through the trial.

MEDICAL THOUGHTS

Diagnosis of cancer. Among all the diseases and illnesses, cancer was probably the most feared. There had been epidemics of polio since the War, TB was constantly in the news, and right now there were outbreaks of typhoid round the country. But cancer was there constantly. Generally, people did not talk about it, it was always hush-hush, and once it was diagnosed, it was generally assumed that no treatments would be of any use.

Likewise the causes were obscure. Mainly it was assumed they were hereditary, and that in fact there were no outside causes of its occurrence. It just came for no good reason, it just happened to you. The idea of an outside agent like tobacco smoking, or excessive sunlight was not yet on the radar.

Still, some early researchers were starting to look for such agents, and were developing tools that would help them in this. Below is a reference to an early effort. It is a long way from the massive machines we use today, but such devices all played their part in throwing some light on the etiology of the dreaded disease.

News item. An optical device equipped with a light and mirrors now enables doctors to look inside their patients' abdomens for signs of disease, three doctors report today.

They say the instrument, known as a peritoneoscope, has shown itself to be valuable in the diagnosis and prognosis of cancer involving organs in the abdominal cavities.

Doctors Samuel Zoeckler, Philip Keil, and George Hegestrom describe their work in peritoneoscopy in the *Journal of the American Medical Association.*

In using the device the doctors make a small incision in the abdomen of the patient, insert the peritoneoscope, and then turn it slowly to light up small areas for viewing through the system of mirrors.

DIY BUCKJUMPING ESSENTIALS

You will remember that when travelling rodeos and Shows came to towns or suburbs, there were always events that involved the thrilling exploitation of horses, and the wild men who rode them. Buckjumping was particularly wild, because it involved the putting of an irritating and hurtful rope round the groin of a horse, and pulling it tight so that the horse would then pig-root and buck about trying to dislodge its rider. This latter daredevil might stay on for ten seconds or less, but if he stayed for longer, it brought the big crowds to their feet. Strangely, looking back, it was not seen by many as cruel and macabre, but rather the price the horse should pay for its otherwise good treatment.

In any case, now, these three Letters add a little to our knowledge of the almost forgotten grand events where "frantic man and wild beast battle for supremacy of the sawdust ring."

Letters, J Gilbert. I was surprised to read a suggestion that buckjump riding is cruel.

Rodeo horses are treated better than many other horses. They are only ridden for about 10 seconds at a time, and the rider is not allowed to strike them **in any way except by the use of spurs**. These are often very fearsome-looking things, but before the rider is allowed on the horse the rowels of the spurs are taped. The horses have to be well fed, so that they will buck their best. Gentlemen riders in show rings are usually rougher on their horses than roughriders. If there were more roughriding and less "hothouse horsemanship", the standard of riding in Australia would be higher.

Letters, 60 YEARS A HORSE-RIDER. I was amused when reading L G D's letter in the discussion on buckjumpers. The idea of describing the crupper as a strap buckled under the horse's tail, and that it causes intense pain, shows to any mind that L G D knows nothing about horses or riding equipment.

The crupper is an essential part of the riding gear to prevent the saddle shifting forward on hilly country, and I can assure you that it causes no pain to the horse.

I know what I am writing about as I have had long experience as a horseman and have been stockman on a station for a long time. But what is downright cruelty and should be stopped by law is the use of a flank rope to make a horse buck.

The flank rope is a device of the devil, and a horse that won't buck without one is not a buckjumper but a trained robot.

Letters, M Oettingen-Ryczy. J Gilbert does not see any cruelty in buckjumping. I should like to see him having to jump with pain. It is not a horse's character to jump in that way. Buckjumping is ugly and senseless, and demonstrates only some monkey agility on the part of the rider.

Look at the faces of rodeo horses, with their ears turned back and nostrils drawn up, dreading the approach of a human being – for humanity and pain are identical to them. These horses are not happy. Riding, whatever kind of riding it is, is only a pleasure if it is a pleasure to the horse.

MARGARETTE SMITH AGAIN

Margarette returned to the fray, and maintained her position. I note a correspondent pointed out that her figures for departures were quite misleading, and that many of those departing intended to return. Still, there were many elements of truth in what she said. I wonder whether she would see us now as being the same or have we changed. For the better?

Letters, Margarette Smith. Some of your writers have raised the question: "Is it the duty of migrants who feel that their European heritage is valuable, to stay and try to instill its rudiments into this remote outpost?"

The answer must be made by every immigrant. If it is "Yes" it presupposes that one believes that Australia can one day develop into a great white civilisation. **But I don't.** I think that its full resources will only be realised eventually when it is incorporated into Asia.

Australians tend to have the unjustified belief that while their own country is in a state of whirling change and development, Europe is resting on the glories of past achievement in a static doze. This is not true. There is precious little "spoon-feeding" in European life to-day; competition in every activity is far stiffer than here, but the atmosphere is alive and stimulating and the standard of achievement is higher.

Hence for me there is greater satisfaction in adding my mite to the struggle for survival and development of the things I value in Europe, where I shall be financially poor, but feel happy and creative; whereas if I remain here I shall be richer, but frustrated by banging my head against the brick wall of Australian conservatism, apathy, or active hostility, and by having a currency which will buy me none of the things that I desire. What is the point of putting my future into a materialistic bubble which I feel will ultimately burst; and can I, in this case, do anything useful by staying?

Incidentally, I notice that the permanent departures for the first six months of 1953 are at a higher rate than the 29,000 of 1952. What about it, Australia? The challenge is yours, as well as the migrants.

Comment. Many migrants who returned to Britain did so because of economic hardship, bitterly bemoaning the fact that the Government had not provided jobs and satisfactory accommodation. Margarette Smith, however, seems to be removed from such "whingeing Poms", and was critical of the aspirations and activities of the people she was forced to live with. It seems to me that she was presenting a middle-class and upper-class view of British society, and that the working classes there had other expressions of culture that were quite different from the forms she sought. In effect, she was thinking about British Culture, rather than British culture.

NEWS AND VIEWS

Letters, Ex Nurse. The demands being made on the Parramatta Mental Hospital nurses stagger me.

I trained at Parramatta Mental Hospital 30 years ago. In Ward 5 we never worked with less than five nurses and on special occasions two extra nurses, and at that time we had 45 to 50 patients in the ward. In Ward 2 (the epileptics' ward) there was a similar staff and always four nurses in Ward 3 and 4. I understand that the number of patients per ward is almost doubled now.

How can patients get care and attention, and how can young girls stand up to the strain of such work? Even 30 years ago the wastage of nurses was high. Of 25 girls commencing first-year lectures, perhaps five would be on the staff at the year's end.

The demand for an average of four nurses per ward should bring every relative of a mental patient to his or her feet in support of the nurses.

Letters, J N Neale. I wish to protest against the poor quality of the "peanut" coke supplied in Sydney today.

Exasperated by clinkers choking my stove I told a friend that I intended to discard it. He suggested treating the coke by putting it in water, whereupon the good fuel would float and the clinkers sink. I did this and easily half the material sank. The rest burns beautifully, but I now realise that with supplies at nine Pounds a ton, I am paying more than 4 Pounds for rubbish.

OCTOBER: POLICE ON THE BEAT

For the last 60 years, Australia has had a love-hate relationship with its Police Forces. For most law-abiding citizens, that is, the vast majority, the police impact rarely into their lives. They might get visits at home for the purpose of checking gun licences, or for issuing rare Court summonses and the like, but these are brief and studiously cordial. Apart from that, they are most likely to have contact over traffic matters, and then relations might get a bit frayed. Still, if a serious crime is committed, most householders turn quickly to the police, and are generally pleasantly surprised at how genuinely professional and sympathetic they are.

I have to add that obviously there are some areas and families and gangs and age-groups that hate the "pigs, and wallopers" and will do so all their lives, and that these people are in a constant battle with them. That, however, does not change my assessment that, for the most part, they are more loved that hated across the community in general.

The following Letters look at how they were viewed sixty-odd years ago. The correspondence opens with a long and thoughtful Letter from a former London officer, where, I understand, relations with the police were about as good as you could get.

Letters, Ex-London "Bobby". As an ex-Metropolitan (London) policeman who has retired in Australia, I have viewed with concern the relationship between police and public during four years in Sydney.

This relationship borders on hostility which is apparent in the number of alleged bashings, untruths and illicit practices attributed to the police and reluctance on the part of the public to assist the police in their civil duties.

In England the Police Force is regarded as a friend and ally of the public, and the police and public work together in mutual good fellowship for the public good. This friendly feeling has done more to solve crimes through "information received" than all the deductions from fingerprints and following of clues. Quite apart from indirect help, the public can always be relied on to give direct help to any constable who is in difficulties.

Today as one of the public, I view with concern the attitude of the police towards the public of this city of Melbourne. As a car driver, I have suffered overbearing rudeness from the police in regard to unintentional errors that I have committed in driving. These remarks have been expressed to me in such terms that had I used the same in my official capacity in London, they would certainly have resulted in a complaint followed by disciplinary action being taken against me. I have seen police on point duty "bawl out" pedestrians in terms which should not be tolerated.

In view of these constant, almost daily, incidents, I am not surprised that the public attitude towards the police is unfriendly.

Further, recent disclosures at a liquor commission, alleged bashings, and a Judge's ruling in regard to the truthfulness of evidence given by a police officer are all incidents that must adversely affect mutual relationship.

In my opinion the Police Force here would be well advised to alter its methods. I suggest that an attitude of tactful authority towards average citizens, and an intelligent firmness towards criminals be adopted. In so doing the efficiency of the police would not suffer, while much good would come of it.

Letters, D C Northam. Lately there has been nothing but criticism of our Police Force, and I have looked in vain for readers' letters defending the fine, unselfish work of police.

We take for granted the fine work they do in floods, droughts, Police Boys' clubs, and rescue work. Hardly a day goes by when we do not read of the police rescuing someone from drowning, or from snow country or bushfires. Yet we repay their courage and efficiency by standing by and doing nothing when they are set on by thugs.

Letters, A M. The contrast which "Ex-London Bobby" draws between the attitude towards the public of London and Sydney police is fully justified.

Four times during the last year or so I have been spoken to by traffic police. On two occasions the police were truculent and provocative in the extreme. Once I was abused in language which, had it been used by me, would probably have landed me in court. On the fourth occasion (strangely, the only one on which I was seriously, though unintentionally, at fault) I was treated with fairness and courtesy.

Some years ago I drove a car in England for the best part of a year. In the first few months I often erred through ignorance, but the police, though they were not aware that I was a struggling stranger, were invariably helpful and understanding. They even addressed me as "Sir."

Here on one occasion I was stopped by the constable shouting "Hey mug, where do you think you're going?"

Letters, Gordon S Fraser, Superintendent of Security, Qantas. Your correspondent "Ex-London Bobby" comments adversely upon traffic police whose patience may have been severely tested by his "unintentional errors."

From his dealings with this minor representation, he criticises the NSW Police Force as a whole. He makes no mention as to whether he has met police officers performing duty in country centres when they are just as much "allies of the public" as their English village counterparts.

"Ex-London 'Bobby" would have no knowledge of the lawless element that commenced to grow in this country during the unfortunate War years when parental control was necessarily absent, weapons were too close to hand, and the influence of certain overseas Servicemen was apparent. This trouble was countered by such organisations as police boys' clubs, coupled with the wise counsel and firm tact of local police officers coming into contact with offenders in their respective districts. A few continued to go wrong, and they were promptly dealt with and today form portion of our present gaol population.

I come more into regular contact with the present-day police forces of the world than probably any other person in the Commonwealth, and feel fully qualified to state that by all standards we have a particularly competent and efficient police body, under capable officers, and we should lend it constructive support rather than destructive criticism.

Letters, Lionel Barrie. I hate Sydney's policemen because they so clearly indicate by offensive language, aggressive manner and threatening expression, their belief that they are not Public servants but masters of the public. I hate them because I've so often seen amiable, unprotesting drunks given the same treatment as that needed to compel a belligerent type to enter a patrol wagon.

I hate them because their apparent carelessness allows so many arrested persons to receive injuries by falling down while in custody.

I am infuriated whenever I see motorists being booked for infringements, which are exactly the same as those continually committed by all types of police vehicles which operate in my locality.

I've laughed as I've watched children outwit previously alerted policemen and thoughtlessly light a bonfire in the street – but I ceased to laugh when the heels of issue boots were ground into my toes in an effort to extract my voluntary statement that I'd played a part in the fire-lighting.

It is acknowledged that the principle of British justice, which decrees the accused innocent until definitely proven otherwise, results in some lawbreakers escaping the consequences of their actions. The same principle prevents substantiation of ugly rumours regarding police behavior – it is impossible to secure proof against those who are trained to detect evidence.

Letters, T Kinkead, Ex-Inspector. Years of intimate association with members of the police force, as a serving member of that body, leave me convinced that the people of this State can have every confidence in the integrity, honesty and efficiency of the service.

In a body of more than 4,000 men, no matter how carefully they may have been selected, an occasional individual may fall short of the high standard demanded, and thus bring discredit on his comrades. The frailty of human nature is universal I would remind your correspondent "ex-London Bobby" that London crowds are more amenable to discipline than their counterpart in Sydney.

While I am not attempting to justify coarse or unseemly language by police to motorists and others, I would say that local-born members of our police force are in a much better position to judge the appropriate language to use to fellow Australians. To address the average citizen as "sir" would be taken as an indication of subserviency or cheap sarcasm, and hold the police up to ridicule.

Our police force is of the people. It is made up of men and women who have the same concepts of liberty and justice as the next person.

Letters, W Ashley-Brown, Archdeacon. In any large body of men there may easily be a few who are bullies by nature or uncouth in address. It would be in the interests of the police force as a whole to disown such black sheep.

But writing as one with more than 30 years' experience in other countries, I am confident that on the whole in the NSW Police we have a magnificent body of Public servants who are a credit to our country and a safeguard to our liberties.

Letters, Sydneysider. It is noticeable that those who condemn the slightest criticism of our police are people who, because they are "public people," meet only with deference from members of the police force.

The present Government has very clearly shown that it will back the police against the public, right or wrong.

The people of this State must tackle this evil seriously and make it clear to Parliament and the police organisation alike, that the police are the servants of the community with the same obligations as other citizens.

Letters, Solicitor. Granting that force is sometimes necessary in order to effect an arrest, the moment a man has been arrested and is in custody, a police cell is all that is required. The use of any force whatsoever ceases to be necessary and is never justified. On the contrary, from that moment onwards, the police are responsible for seeing that no harm comes to the arrestee.

Depart from that principle and what happens? Suppose the police believe an arrested man to be guilty but they cannot yet prove it. They need a confession to complete their case. Laying aside their "kid gloves", they can obtain it. Under cross-examination in court they necessarily have to deny the use of force when obtaining the confession, and so perjury enters into the case.

Once a police officer has stepped on to that slippery path he can soon find another, by giving evidence of verbal confessions which were never made at all. It is the thin end of the wedge. To the extent that violence of any kind enters the CIB, to however slight a degree, so surely does justice depart from our courts.

Comment. Solicitors' mention of the CIB (in all States) will remind many readers that over the years the reputation of the CIB (or CID), more so than any other Branch of the Force, has had some bad patches, and a few officers therein had gained a reputation for abuse of power and corruption. On the other hand, "police on the beat" have probably enhanced their reputation, and police in the rural areas have maintained their status as equivalent to the best of London's exalted Bobbies.

For the most part, it seems that attitudes have not changed much. The bad things were then apparent, and the good things were as well. It depends, maybe, on where you sit in the vast continuum from lawless to law-abiding. All I can add is that if you are reading this book, I believe you are not likely to have a bad police experience in the near future, so I suggest it is 'wise to keep it that way.

LADDERS IN NYLONS

Most of Australia's nylon stockings in 1953 were made in Australia, though the thread was imported mainly from America. Prior to 1947, our sheerest fashion stockings here were made from silk and these were manufactured from thread that measured 45 denier. When the nylon arrived, thread size started at 45 denier, but fell rapidly to 30 and could now be purchased at 15 denier. Obviously, more problems come with the thinner threads, but still by now, in 1953, 70 per cent of Australian stockings produced are made of 15 denier thread.

None of theses numbers meant much to the women writing below. After the initial complaining Letter, more and more flooded in, and the few below are a small sample of all those published.

Letters, (Mrs) F Mansell. Can there possibly be a conspiracy by nylon manufacturers to produce as many fragile stockings as they can?

There is a genuine grievance among women over the poor quality of the goods now on the market, and fury mounts when stockings tear after one or two days' wear. Yet it was claimed by manufacturers that nylon stockings would be the strongest, longest-wearing, etc., etc. type ever made.

Husbands, I imagine, would not be so eager to admire the "female leg divine" if they realised what part of their income was being spent in maintaining its appearance.

Letters, Mrs A Wilkinson. I agree with what Mrs Mansell wrote about the poor durability and quality of nylon stockings.

Almost every time I put on a pair I find snags or ladders in them, though sometimes they last for three days' wear. I always wear a pair of thin gloves to put them on, so that my short nails or bits of skin on the tips of the fingers do not catch on them.

It is to be hoped that manufacturers will do something about this before women decide to do without nylons. Young people can tan their legs, which looks most attractive in summer.

Letters, Fair Go. I agree with Mrs Mansell that nylon stockings are expensive rubbish.

After reading the manufacturer's advice to wear 25 denier for everyday wear, I tried it, and found that these thicker stockings twist round the leg and one finds the heel in the middle of the instep in a very short while.

There is only one thing for us women to do, if we have any commonsense: don't buy any more.

Letters, Irate. It is not only the finer stockings which ladder on the first or second wearing, as claimed by the Secretary of the Hosiery Makers and Merchants' Association, but 35 denier nylons as well.

I have for years worn an Australian brand of 35 denier nylons which used to last me for months, but the last three pairs, bought recently, have laddered the first day. On comparing these later nylons with the earlier, there seems to be a difference in the manufacture – a tighter weave and a shorter stocking.

Letters, Charlotte Richman. The blame for the nylon stocking situation lies primarily at the door of the Federal Government.

Until about a year ago I was able to purchase first-quality service weight nylons for about 7/11 a pair and sheer nylons for as little as 10/- a pair. These were imported hosiery of superior quality.

Owing to import restrictions, these imported nylons have practically disappeared from the stores, and the few that are available are considerably more expensive in consequence of the "dumping duty"' recently imposed. One can only conclude that a few local manufacturers are being unfairly protected at the expense of the hundreds of thousands of women of this country.

Letters, (Mrs) I Bell. It is gratifying that women are at last realising the wicked waste of money involved in the purchase of nylon stockings.

My daughter, aged 15, like all her friends, insists on nylons for "out of school" wear. It takes two hours of casual typing, for which I am paid 5/- an hour, to buy a 9/11 pair of nylons, which ladder usually on the second or third wearing.

Schoolgirls refuse to wear laddered stockings and, on my daughter's suggestion, I recently purchased her a pair of "mesh" nylons at 16/11, thinking they would give more wear, but although they do not "ladder," they go into holes very easily. I, myself, wear the cast-off laddered stockings, or go without.

Letters, E A. The contention that women wear the wrong nylons for the occasion is not altogether correct, as most women understand the meaning of the different denier now, and few would wear sheer stocking for hard wear or for sport.

I have found 30 denier are no tougher than the more exotic variety. Grass brushing against the ankles on suburban footpaths will soon snag the 30-denier type, and the ladders run just as fast in them as in the sheerest of stockings.

It is no use saying "go without them," as most women do not feel dressed without stockings.

Letters, Paula. As a hard-working business woman of good average build I have found that it pays to buy stockings at least an inch larger than recommended for shoe fittings.

Nylons will not stretch readily and as soon as strain is put upon them they ladder. I wear all deniers and get excellent wear when I purchase the larger sizes. Let some of your correspondents be not ashamed to ask for larger hose.

Letters, H B. Your correspondent "J D" has "a huge pile of useless stockings."

If she will select the good ones out of this pile and put them in a vessel and cover them with cold water, bring them slowly to the boil, and boil slowly for about three-quarters of an hour, she will find that they will be all the same shade and good for further use.

WHITE LEGHORNS ON DISPLAY

Almost every suburb and largish town across Australia had a Bowling Club, and at those hallowed sites many men of senior years congregated on Saturday and Wednesday afternoons for a game of bowls. On Sunday afternoons, the women were allowed in, and normally they also had a run on one afternoon during the week. The ladies, and they were most certainly ladies, were quite mature, were very proper on the surface at least, and were always conspicuous for being well dressed.

Here, by saying "well dressed", I am not implying that they were fashionably dressed. Nor that they were colourful or daring in a quiter way. Quite the contrary in fact. They were well clothed in a standard uniform that was indeed very proper and, some might say, designed to deter any covetous looks that might otherwise have come their way. The wearing of the uniform was strictly policed and woe betide anyone who did not conform.

This uniform, if I remember correctly, was a fully white frock from about two feet below the knees, up to six inches above their clavicles. Long sleeved of course, with white flat-soled shoes and white 70-denier stockings, and a flat hat with a badge of the State Association on it. Many unkind people at the time imagined that they looked like a breed of white hens, and were unkind enough to refer to them as such.

Periodically, some women spoke out against this imposed drabness, but found that many more of their colleagues had their reasons for retaining it. Below is a brief encounter around this subject.

Letters, Mrs E Cameron. Recently a group of women bowlers boarded a train at Central, and I noted with some curiosity the outfit worn, which brought amused and somewhat pitying glances from some of the other passengers.

Their hats could not grace any style of hairdo, and the white cotton stockings and shoes do their very worst for all kinds of ankles. Taken all round, there is a lumpy middle-aged look about the whole ensemble.

Have women bowlers no wish to preserve feminine charm, or are they obliged by some antique rules to wear this unbecoming uniform? Even youngish players contrive to look most forbidding.

What would be wrong with a pleated dress (with or without sleeves) – designed with a waist-line – smart shoes, standard denier suntan stockings – all topped by a white hat of becoming and adaptable shape?

Many women would be attracted to the game if they felt that they would not be the butt of affectionate but slightly humorous remarks from friends and relatives.

Letters, M Southwell. Instructions on what to wear are given by the Women Bowlers' Association.

There has been much distress in clubs regarding the white stockings. Members are ordered to wear them or not play.

I have seen a woman on the bowling green with a visiting team wearing short sleeves. She was told to put on her long-sleeved cardigan to cover her arms, otherwise she would not be allowed to play.

Letters, V Froud. I would like to reply to Mrs Cameron on the dress of women bowlers.

Imagine trying to deliver a bowl correctly on a windy day in a pleated skirt. It could not be done. As for a fashionable shoe, we can only wear flat rubber soles. Many of our members are past their prime, but still good bowlers. They could not wear short sleeves. Most of us wear nylon stockings, not cotton. We go on to the green to enjoy friendship and play the game, not to worry about looking glamorous.

Comment. Over the years, the requirement to wear a uniform at formal matches has been preserved. Skirts can be a little shorter, and colours can be used by certain players. Styles are more generous than before. The policing of uniforms is still done, though probably no more than in other sports.

The big change in womens's bowling has been the influx of younger women. Many relative youngsters have joined up, and also a fair number of deliberate athletes who see this as a sport that can bring them personal success. Also changed is the attitude that somehow the sport was a private enclave for chosen women. Right now, you can turn on TV most Saturday afternoons and see an international match, played by young women who are clearly close to professional status. his is all done with the approval of the various State Associations that are now thriving on the publicity that TV brings to the sport.

THE QUEEN'S ENGLISH

Pronunciation of the Queen's English. The Australian Broadcasting Commission (ABC) radio, was modelled on a grander service in Britain, the BBC, and had remained in its shadow for 20 years. As a nation, we took many of our News Services directly from the Old Country, and also many feature articles, commentaries and serials.

As well as that, many of the announcers spoke with a very definite BBC accent. Put in Oz terms, this was a posh Pommie plum-in-the-mouth way of speaking, far removed from the rough nasal Australian commonly heard here. On some formal occasions, this sounded acceptable, but as many writers below pointed out, there were some utterances that challenged the listeners.

Letters, J G Reed. It would need the phonetic alphabet of "Pygmalion's" Professor Higgins to do justice to the mealy-mouthed murdering of our mother tongue indulged by both national and commercial station announcers.

Old as well as New Australians must have wondered whether the Swiss Navy was no longer fiction, but fact, to hear of wharf-Laborer trouble at "Berne" (Bowen, Qld.).

Weather information concerning "lairt shahs falling at Naara on the sarth kerst," or chronicling of a suicide when "a woman's buddy was fahnd flirting in the harbour," have been beaten only by an announcer who informed listeners that "Oozhong Ermandy would conduct the Than Hurl Erkistrah."

There is no excuse for this vowel-fouling speech. A copy of Professor Nicklin's *Sounds of Standard English* should be a "must" in every broadcasting studio, while CN Bayertz's excellent recorded series *Spoken English* – prepared by an Australian company – deserves to be played to all announcers as an example of pleasing and melodious speech to which they should all aspire.

Letters, Anne Martin. It is the actual tone of the voices on the ABC which people object to.

When a woman announcer says, "This is the BBC" and a man says "Hare is the nuse" it is sickening.

No matter if it is "educated Australian" or "King's English," if the announcer has not a clear natural voice with a sincere unaffected sound, it certainly is painful to listen to.

Letters, Ian Wynne. It would be interesting to know when your correspondent J Reed heard an announcer say that "Oozhong Ermandy would conduct the Than Hurl Erkistrah."

There is not, nor has there ever been in Australia, an orchestra known as the Town Hall Orchestra, and the last time that Eugene Ormandy conducted any orchestra in this country was in 1944.

Mr Reed's imagination is perhaps better developed than his memory or his sense of hearing.

There were plenty of similar letters, and I have extracted below some of the phrases that were found offensive. I wish you well in de-cyphering them.

The Air Beer Seer. The country town of Carra. The time is noine minutes to noine

The days of the week are Mundee, Chuzedee, Wenzdee, through to Satterdee. We all live in Erstralia rand New Zealand, on the Sarth Kerst.

Comment. Well, I am pleased they got that straightened out. One interesting tit-bit was a comment in one Letter that read "I might respectfully suggest that the annoying announcers model themselves on young James Dibble, whose speech is clear and unaffected." This is the same James Dibble who, over thirty years, read the news so well and professionally in the prime spot on ABC radio and television, and who died only in 2010, at the age of 87.

NEWS AND TRIVIA

Dingo-proof fence. News item. Queensland will legislate this session for a 3,200-mile dingo-proof fence to enclose Queensland's main sheep area. The Minister for Lands, Mr T Foley, announced after a Cabinet meeting tonight that the United Graziers' Association had approved the Government's plan.

The fence will link up with the NSW dingo-proof fence west of Hungerford, Queensland. Then it will extend to the north and swing in a wide arc almost to the Northern Territory border. It is estimated that dingoes kill half a million sheep a year and cost the wool industry 2 million Pounds a year. The annual cost of dingo bonuses is about 70,000 Pounds.

NOVEMBER: THE MELBOURNE CUP

The running of a horse race crops up every year at about this time. It is called the Melbourne Cup. I know that as a patriot I am supposed to enthuse over this event, and so normally give it some grudging mention, and poke a little bit of fun at it. This year, however, I will treat it seriously and give you one page of breathless cover.

This is the 92nd consecutive time that the Cup has been run, over a two mile course. There were nearly 500 entries this year, but these have been whittled down to 30 starters.

The prize money totals 14,000 Pounds, of which the winner gets 10,000 Pounds. Entry fee is 77 Pounds per horse, though the preparation for the race involves an average of 500 Pounds, a small fortune.

One favourite nag this year is called Hydrogen. It runs on all four legs and carries a jockey on racing days. He wears clothes that he would not be seen dead in if the horse wasn't there to carry him out of trouble. Other horses will run as well, and maybe a few might be faster. Thousands and thousands of fans will still be sober enough to watch the race from the stands, and will have a smashing day.

But that's all I can do. I have run out of enthusiasm, and will only get worse if I keep going.

COMPULSORY UNIONISM PLUS

The NSW Labor Government had recently been re-elected, and was ruling with a comfortable majority. It had been in power virtually since the War and much of its success came from its close association with the Trade Unions. These latter groups were all run by a small coterie of fervent believers in Socialism of one sort or another, were firmly against any compromise with capitalists and big business, and were generally opposed to effecting changes by negotiation. Some of them were far enough "left" to be called Communists, and some of them were bullies of their own members, and were prone to use violence to encourage employees to become members of the Union.

The average worker was, by 1953, a member of his Union. Not that he was interested in Union affairs, but he did believe that over the years, Unions and the Labor Party had protected the workers from the most excessive demands of capitalism, and he saw them as the ultimate back-stop if problems arose in the workplace. But having said that, most members were **not conscious of the formation of Union policies**. They simply went on strike when the Union rep told them to do so. And they paid their not inconsiderable fees to belong to the Union.

The Executives of the Unions thus were able, unfettered by popular member resistance, to decide Union policies, and in particular, to combine together to influence the policies of the State Government. It fact, by 1953, the Government in NSW was so reliant on this Union support that it was said ad nauseum that the Unions ran the Government.

NEW LEGISLATION

At the end of October, the NSW Government announced that it intended to make draconian changes to the laws affecting Trade Unions. Among other major provisions, the new laws would extend the scope of the Industrial Arbitration Act to include persons in managerial positions, and not just the "workers" under them.

Then it proposed that Union delegates should have unrestricted right of entry to working places and company records relating to employment. Further, **that all "workers" must join a Union within 28 days**, and that they could not continue in employment if they did not.

Employers who hired non-unionists would be fined. On top of that , it decreed that where fines were imposed for violations of the new laws, then half of the revenue would go to the Trade Unions.

Definitions were added or changed. A "worker" was defined as a person who earned less than 2,000 Pounds a year. Doctors and similar professionals were exempted from the provisions, as were shopkeepers. Executives working for companies were to also be exempted if they earned over 2,000 Pounds, but they were included if they earned less.

OPPOSITION TO THE NEW LEGISLATION

One of the main opponents of the legislation was the Editor of the *SMH*. From 23rd October till the end of November he wrote five Editorials, each criticising some aspect of the new measures. For example, in his first missive he pointed out that the UN Declaration of Human Rights states that "No person may be compelled to belong to an Association", and that non-unionists now had a month to join or be sacked. He added that the Premier Joe Cahill had just been re-elected last February, but he had made no mention of this legislation at that time. "He asked the people to trust the Labor Government, and they did. Now they are getting their reward."

There were plenty of other critics. In November the *SHM* published 100 Letters on the matter, and 95 of these were critical of the new laws. On November 18th, the paper published 12 Letters, and the Editor then added "These are a selection of views from the large number of Letters which the *Herald* has received on the subject. Unfortunately there is space only for a very small proportion of the total."

I too have problems here with space. I have room for only a handful of Letters, so I have included a selection that demonstrates just a few different points. I stress, though, that there was enough Letter response to make perhaps fifty different points and attitudes.

Letters, E S Owens. I wonder how long it will be before premiums for membership charged and dues sky-rocket if the projected legislation for virtually compulsory unionism becomes an established fact?

The evils of the press gangs of old pale beside the possibilities of compulsory unionism. And just imagine the growth and cost of union management when it is drunk with this power!

Letters, V Collins. The bludgeoning of citizens into organisations for which they have no regard is an act of dictatorship for which the Cahill Government has no mandate. Mr J T Lang was dismissed by the Governor of the day for behaviour far less radical than that of the present Government.

Letters, (Ald.) Trevor Humphries. Is it asking too much of the Government to let the people vote on its compulsory unionism proposals? Surely no measure which affects the lives of the people as vitally as this should be sprung upon them without their being able to give any expression of opinion whatever.

As one member of the much-abused populace of New South Wales, I am tired of the Cahill Government's indifference to the rights of the public.

Letters, O D Bissett. In all Mr Nairn's rather specious arguments he misses the main point.

It is notorious that the trade-unions are an integral part of the Labor Party. Their time, their officials, their offices, their whole organisations, to say nothing of their funds, are continually used in support of the Labor Party. To advocate that people should be forced in order to keep their jobs to join an organisation which works in unremitting support of a political party – any political party – is extremely obnoxious and objectionable.

Letters, D A Herbrand. In small one-man businesses, such as smallgoods, grocers, tobacconists, pastrycooks, libraries, jewelers, artisans, plumbers and all the various trades, dressmakers, milliners, etc, the proprietor is assisted by his wife or son or daughter, in many cases having the benefit of their full employment. Add in 50,000 wives and sons and daughters on the farms across the State. They work as partners, but not as a legal partnership with all its legal complications.

These small businesses operate rather as a family unit, because the family is dependent on the income from that business, and while the proprietor no doubt pays at least the award salary to any sons or daughters on his payroll, the matter of strict hours is very often overlooked, and there is a certain amount of give and take.

Does the bill for compulsory unionism mean that every member of his family who will now have to join a union? Does it mean also that if the wife or daughter gives a "helping hand" for two or three hours, she will have to be paid at the casual rate of the ordinary award rate? Does it mean that if the union for any reason whatever, however paltry, calls its members out on strike, the wife and son and daughter have to line up with the oppressed workers against the husband (who now stands in the position of the hated capitalist and oppressor of the workers)? And will they have to stand aside while they see the business crumble due to their impotence to help the business carry on?

Will the family members who will not strike be branded (forever) as scabs?

Letters, L Smith. I object strongly to the use of the term "parasite" in a letter under the signature of the secretary of the ALP Youth Council.

There are tens of thousands of these "parasites" in New South Wales who have never sought any assistance from unions and do not seek it now. They are well able to stand on their own feet and in most cases their earnings are well above award rates.

Letters, Clive S Liston. What is the citizen to do when the union orders an illegal strike? What is his position if he obeys the arbitration laws and stays at work? Can the union dismiss him for this or any other law-abiding action? What happens in the event of political strikes? What if a union delegate and a worker have a fight? The Union will ban the worker, and he will lose his job.

Union leaders would do better if they considered honestly why so many do not join their unions. Apart from those who are merely apathetic, there is a large group who find the general outlook, principles and methods of the average union most distasteful, although they may support its more reasonable aims. They would be quite happy to stay outside the awards gained by the unions, and rely on their own initiative, training and experience to reach agreement with employers on wages and conditions.

SUPPORTING THE LEGISLATION

Comment. There were not many Letters published supporting the legislation. Of course, it is possible to suspect that the *SMH* was deliberately suppressing those Letters that spoke against a cause that it was obviously supporting. But its record on fairness had stood the test of time, and it seems wrong to suspect Editorial intervention.

The paucity of these few Letters, compared to the abundance of those above, tells its own story. It was clear from all indications that this legislation was unpopular. This of course proves nothing. Many Governments are forced at times to enact laws that would not initially gain public support. In this case, it would have hoped that in practice many of the forecasts of doom would be proven wrong. After all, New Zealand and Queensland had lived with compulsion for years.

By the end of November, the legislation was all tidied up and passed into law. The obvious thing to look for after that was an elector back-lash at the next elections. However, the result at the next election was just **a small drop in the Labor Party vote**, and so it appears there was no lasting legacy of this bitter dispute. But we will keep an eye on it next month.

Letters, Allan Hardie. Much has been published about the violation of personal liberties involved in compulsory unionism. But in a community such as ours, should an employee, enjoying the benefit of and concessions granted by an industrial award, have the personal liberty to impose on his fellow workers by accepting the fruits of their organisation and exertions on their common behalf, without feeling under an obligation in any way to contribute, financially or otherwise, to that organisation?

Such individuals as do evade their responsibilities in this regard usually shelter behind the knowledge that there cannot be two awards, one for unionists and another for non-unionists.

Award concessions do not fall like manna from the skies. They are won only by hard work and agitation, and necessitate a full-time secretary together with staff and office equipment. And the latter in turn require to be financed by those who will benefit by them, namely, the employees in an enterprise themselves.

To me the matter is not a political one, but one for one's own conscience to decide. And it is unfortunate that those who cannot be influenced by a moral sanction have to be confronted with a legal one.

I have belonged to the Liberal Party, or to its counterpart, ever since I first became entitled to vote; but I have also belonged to my "union", the Metropolitan Board of Water Supply and Sewerage Salaried Officers' Association, ever since I as a lad of 16 succeeded to the right to earn my own living.

Nor is it correct to say that a union **has** to support the Labor Party. The control of a union and its funds is still in its members; and the Liberal and Country Parties have striven to give the rank and file the control. It is for the members themselves to decide what, if any, party they will support.

THE QUEEN'S VISIT

Her Majesty, Queen Elizabeth II, had decided to make a Royal Visit to Australia early next year. This was good news for the millions of ordinary people who fervently supported the monarchy and all the other manifestations of the British Empire. They had been disappointed 18 months earlier when intended visits had been cancelled because of the unexpected death of King George VI. Now, however, the newly-crowned Queen was to visit these golden shores and, early though it might be, all sorts of people were making preparations.

News item. November 11. The NSW Premier, Joe Cahill, said last night that the official street decoration scheme for the Royal Tour is for 1,203 colourful standards, and costing 22,650 Pounds. The official 30ft high standards would encircle the perimeter of the main city, and include all cross streets from Bridge to Liverpool Streets. Some of the banners would be of the maypole type, and have 40 yards of material. More traditional standards would have a regal finial in the form of a crown or spearpoint, with a heraldic design embossed on the base of the banner.

He added that an offer had been received from a Sydney firm to lend a giant lion-and-dragon emblem which it had acquired from the Coronation decorations. It weighed one ton. "If we can, we will erect this over the toll gates of the Harbour Bridge, and will floodlight it at night."

Comment. Oh goodie. Another big pomp-ous occasion.

Letters, R Ballhause, Wellington Teachers. For the Queen's visit to Dubbo next year, it is anticipated that more than 11,000 children will be assembled on the Dubbo Oval.

Of these over 6,000 will be travelling, mostly by train, from all over the vast expanses of western NSW. Large numbers will have paid considerable sums in fares, and will have been in trains, in the hot, western summer for up to 14 hours during the day - a most arduous experience for an adult, let alone crowds of children.

Yet in order that adequate time can be devoted to the hierarchy of officialdom, it appears that the children are to be delegated to a subordinate position with a time allocation of only 8 minutes out of two hours.

Members of the Wellington Teachers' Association at their last meeting expressed disgust at these latest arrangements. They consider their opinions reflect those of the majority of people in western N.S.W. when they request that the 11,000 children be given **a major part in the Dubbo welcome,** and also that they be given an opportunity of hearing as well as seeing the Queen at their assembly.

SOME NEWS AND TRIVIA

Letters, E Merryfull. I read with interest "Kanangra's" article on the heavy sheep losses being caused by what he calls "dingoes." I wish to point out that the animal in the published picture, described as "a full-grown dingo in captivity," is definitely a cross-bred.

The only resemblance to a pure-bred is in the head. Otherwise the animal shown is too high, too long, and has a huskie's tail. The pure dingo tail is very short, with a heavy brush carried straight where the photograph shows the animal to have a ring tail.

I lived many years in dingo country, caring for puppies, and saw many attempts to domesticate them. I venture to say that at the present time we have not one pure-bred dingo in NSW.

Some time ago, when the question of cross-breeding between dingoes and Alsatians arose, a move was made to have all Alsatians sterilised. The then Minister for Agriculture, Mr Main, agreed to have the remains of a dingo shot at Armidale brought to Sydney for three experts, of whom I was one, to examine.

Our investigation proved that the dog was a mixture of dingo, collie and staghound, but with no Alsatian. We found that the only pure-bred dingo in NSW was the one brought from Queensland for the Taronga Park Zoo.

Whatever the breeding of these animals, their nuisance value is the same, and the matter of their extermination or control is one which the Commonwealth government should treat with urgency before they do any further damage to the wool industry.

Letters, 45 Years A Pipe Smoker. It is high time smokers demanded something better from the tobacco manufacturers than the stuff they are handing out.

I am an Australian, and a staunch supporter of Australian products, but, like others, require full value for my money, both in quantity and quality. When I want timber I go to a timber merchant, when I want twine I go to a jute merchant, but lately I find it is possible to obtain both from the tobacconists by purchasing certain local brands of pipe tobacco.

Imported tobaccos are evidently packed under much stricter supervision overseas than is the case here.

A PERSONAL MEMORY

In 1953, I was in my second year at Sydney University. One subject I took was Geology II. Within that, there was a strand on exploration and the geology pertaining to it.

In lectures, we had been told time and again that Oz geology was hopeless for oil. Something about Permian rocks and synclines and upthrusts. Whatever it was, we had all learned it verbatim, and were delighted to see an exam question that asked "Will oil ever be discovered in Australia?" We poured our set-piece answers out triumphantly onto the exam papers.

At the end of the exam, we walked out of the Great Hall, and newspapers and newsboys blurted at us "Oil Struck at Exmouth Gulf", off the coast of WA. And it truly was. Too late. Who cared? No one really. Exams were over.

WHO IS OUR PRIME CHRISTIAN LEADER?

When the Queen makes it to our shores, there will be lots of ceremonies attended by clergymen for all Christian Churches. Some readers might expect that these men of God will just push and shove to see who gets closest to the Queen, and will have a footrace to see who gets there first. But those readers would be wrong.

In fact, the order of precedence has been determined by the Commonwealth, using a criterion that is guaranteed to promote controversy among all except the winners.

First of all, be it noted that there is no "established" Church in Australia. In Britain, they have the Church of England and there is no dispute over precedence. One other criterion that could be used would be the number of adherents. Then it would come down to a two-horse race, with the C of E and the Catholics as the only runners.

But that is a bit tricky, because there is a High C of E and a Low. Normally, they are reluctant to be lumped together. Then again, the Catholics have more people attend church every Sunday than does the C of E. Maybe they deserve first prize.

The decision made was to give primacy to the church with **the longest serving temporal head at the time**.

In this case, Pope Pius XII romped it in, so the Catholics got the top barrier position.

DECEMBER: GOODIES FROM OVERSEAS

10 HIT SONGS FROM AMERICA

That's Amore	Dean Martin
The Doggie in the Window	Patti Page
Side by Side	Kay Starr
Stranger in Paradise	Tony Bennett
Three Coins in a Fountain	Frank Sinarta
Young at Heart	Frank Sinarta
Your Cheatin' Heart	Frankie Lane
Ev'rybody Loves Saturday Night	Glenn Campbell
Goodnight, Sweetheart	Calvin Carter
Rock Around the Clock	Jimmy de Knight

10 MOVIES RELEASED

Peter Pan	Cartoon
The Robe	Burton, Simmons
Here to Eternity	Clift, Lancaster
Shane	Ladd, Arthur
Marry a Millionaire	Monroe, Grable
Gentlemen Prefer Blondes	Monroe, Russell
Mogambo	Gable, Gardner
Salome	Rita Hayworth
Roman Holiday	Peck, Hepburn
Julius Caesar	Marlon Brando

ACADEMY AWARDS:

Best Actor: William Holden (Stalag 17)

Best Actress: Audrey Hepburn (Roman Holiday)

Best Movie: From Here To Eternity

THE KOREAN WAR

The fighting thankfully was over. Sadly, though, the folly that had marred the last two years, continued on. Soldiers were slowly being sent home, prisoners were being slowly repatriated, trenches were being filled with soil, air-fields were being abandoned as you might expect. But no real progress was being made towards working out the future of the two halves of Korea. All sorts of conferences were being held, Swedish UN workers were going on strike, India was demanding to be heard at the peace table, America was giving the Reds "the last chance to come to heel" every week, and the Reds were being obdurate.

It was all just going on and on, and it continued that way into the New Year, then it just went on and on some more, and slowly it ended up with what we have now. Two nations that before the war were one, were now bitterly divided by a neutral zone along the 38th Parallel, with enormous ideological differences keeping them apart. What a disaster.

Comment. I have now written 28 of the 30 books in this series. In a moment of madness that I allow myself at the end of most books, I will get off the fence I have been carefully sitting on, and give you my unedited fair dinkum opinion. Here it is: I have seen two events in the 14 years that drove me to despair. The first was the sending of Anzac troops into Greece and then Crete in 1941. What a terrible loss of life for a cause that was at best hopeless.

The second was the Korean War from go to whoa. No one can remember what excuse was given for its start, but everyone knew it was a punch-up between Capitalism and Communism, to be fought for propaganda purposes, in a region far away from their own shores. It was marked all the way by ineptitude and incompetence, and now at the end everyone was still messing round pushing their own little barrows, with no concern for the welfare of anyone living in either of the two states created. Like I said, what a disaster.

COMPULSORY UNIONISM

The enabling legislation passed through the NSW Parliament at the end of November. This did not mean however that the opposition to it died down. In fact, it came from everywhere. The employers immediately announced that they would challenge it in the Supreme Court. They thought they could do that by mid-January, but they carelessly forgot that this nation closed down for the whole of January, so they had to delay for a month. In the meantime, their great propagandist, the *Sydney Morning Herald* kept up its vitriolic editorial attacks, and greatly influenced the public through its Letters columns.

On top of that, many Unions had second thoughts. For example, the various waterside Unions wanted to keep their "closed shops" that meant newcomers were generally stopped from working on the wharves. Any new jobs went to their families and friends. They saw the new laws as dangerous to that cause. The ordinary Unionist saw no need for the law, and that it imposed many unwanted restraints and costs on them. Mothers and sons and daughters who helped out on farms and in shops were very frightened by the thought that their family could lose income through strikes and, even worse, that they might be labelled as scabs for the rest of their lives. The clergy also contributed, and sermon after sermon denounced the "Communist inspired monopolistic scheme."

Before the Court case was decided, the Government was having second thoughts. For example, it had stated that employees had only 28 days to join a Union. Now they said that rule would not be enforced, and the period would be extended. It never did say what the period would become. Then its feet got colder as more and more anomalies in the laws were pointed out. By the time the Court case had been decided, it was in full retreat. In fact, believe it or not, it never did enforce the legislation. In effect, it was replaced in 1959 by a variation which provided that Union members would get preference over non-members if they had equal qualifications for a job. But even that was pointless because, under existing rules, it was always easy to fix the qualifications so that the person, whom the Union preferred, had the best paper qualifications or personal skills.

Comment. Compulsory Unionism as proposed in 1953 turned out to be a complete fizzer. Getting off the fence again, for the last time, I would have liked to have seen the Labor Government punished at the next election for its illiberal concept, and its inept execution of its plan. But the electors did not see it this way, and simply reduced the Government's seats by half a dozen. And that just cut the majority from huge, down to very large.

THE QUEEN *IS* COMING, HURRAH HURRAH

Her Majesty and Consort were now in the Pacific sailing a leisurely course though Tonga and Fiji, to New Zealand, with suitable greetings and ceremonies at those places. In New Zealand, the gloss was taken off her tour a little by a tragic event just after Christmas, when a bridge over a ravine collapsed during a flood. A train en route from Wellington to Auckland was on it at the time, and when the train plunged into the valley and waters below, 166 lives were lost.

Here in Australia, things were warming up in preparation. As you would expect, many different forces were at work to make it a success or to gratify varying ambitions. Below is a sample.

Press release. Under the heading *Parks Will be Gay for Royalty,* the Director of Parks announced a comprehensive program for Sydney's Hyde Park.

For example, City Council staff men are at work on some of the preparations for special displays in Hyde Park during the Royal visit. The decoration and illumination scheme will be the most elaborate ever carried out there. At night the park will be completely floodlit. Above the flower beds, small hooded lights, placed below eye level to prevent glare, will illuminate the flowers. All lights will be clear except the coloured ones playing on the water of the Archibald Fountain. The Sydney County Council will carry out the lighting.

The Sandringham sunken garden near the corner of Park and College Streets (Melbourne) will be remodelled by the end of this year. The main change there will be the erection of the State memorials to King George V and King George VI. These will take the form of two wrought metal gates, incorporating heraldic designs, flanked by two stone walls. One wall will bear in simple lettering the name "King George V," the other "King George VI."

The present pool in the garden will be remodelled, and will be given a new ceramic floor with a design representing Australian fauna. Twenty-five small jets of water will rise from the pool.

Comment. Such preparations all over the city would doubtless add to the gaety of the occasions.

Letters, W Chas Crawford. I noticed recently that the VCs were to be brought to Sydney on the occasion of the Queen's visit.

Another section, not of our immediate community, is certainly entitled to similar consideration. I refer to those wonderful men in the islands who became celebrated as "Coast Watchers."

Letters, Nature Lover. How are we to make the landscape as beautiful as possible for the Royal progress through the streets?

Householders along the routes are giving their homes a face-lift with bright paint; the gayest plants are being set out in the gardens; streets, homes and gardens are being tidied and decorated to honour the Queen; but what is being done about the billboards?

Is it possible to have beautiful billboards?

To quote Ogden Nash:
I think that I shall never see
A billboard lovely as a tree.
Perhaps unless the billboards fall,
I'll never see a tree at all.

Letters, MacLeod Morgan. One can only view with amazement the Premier's decision that the Queen will not now proceed by the Lawrence Hargrave Drive on her return from Wollongong, due, we are told, to the risk of "falling stones" from the cliffs between Scarborough and Coalcliff.

It would seem, then, that numbers of the Queen's subjects hour by hour, day by day, week by week are jeopardising their lives in their use of this road – but they are still sound of limb!

The decision will deprive many hundreds of loyal citizens of the upper South Coast of the means of conveniently saluting their Sovereign, and incidentally deprive our Sovereign of some unique scenery and .a view of the site of the discovery in Australia during the eighteenth century of coal, one of our greatest primary industries today.

Letters, H G. There is every justification for altering the route by which the Queen will be driven by motor from Wollongong.

The beauty of the coast is not marked in the vicinity of Scarborough, and Coalcliff, and it should be realised that the danger of falling stones applies not only to the Royal visitors but to the number of spectators who doubtless would line the roadway there.

The Queen will see plenty of coastal scenery without travelling on this stretch, which has an impressive seascape, but a some what depressing land frontage.

Letters, F Wilmot. On the eve of the arrival of her Majesty at Tonga, perhaps the following episode might interest your readers.

It was in 1915, and I was the gunnery officer of the first ship in the Royal Australian Navy that fired a shot in anger. This was at the taking of Rabaul from the Germans.

I was lent to the RAN from the Royal Navy. We were sent by the Admiralty to Tonga, as at that time we were anxious to keep on friendly terms, as we did not want the risk of perhaps German ships, possibly submarines, operating from there.

It is a beautiful harbour, and on our arrival we fired a salute of 21 guns for her Majesty the Queen of Tonga who, I think, is the same lady that rules over the island at the present time.

I noticed two guns on the hill above us, but there was no reply to our salute.

About half an hour afterwards a boat came off with a letter to our captain asking us if we could kindly lend 21 rounds of ammunition to return the salute.

We duly obliged!

ROYAL BALLS

Victoria's arrangements for two Royal balls would not be cancelled, the director of the State Royal Tour Committee, Mr. W. Jungwirth, said tonight. He was commenting on a New Zealand report that Australian Royal Tour authorities should strike all State balls from the Royal tour programme.

The New Zealand Royal Tour Director said yesterday that no ball was included in the New Zealand programme because the Queen herself had told him she preferred to have them left out. He said no suggestion had been made that Victoria should cancel the Governor's Ball and a civic ball which had been planned. If a request was received, he said, it would be communicated to the States and undoubtedly the Queen's wish would be acceded to.

In NSW, a ball has been arranged for February 5 – the Lord Mayor's Ball, at the Town Hall.

A DEVIATION: THE QUEEN'S ENGLISH

I remarked earlier that sometimes an innocuous Letter on a simple subject could stir enough passions to cause a flurry of Letters. Here below we have another example of this on a matter as important as the use of the Queen's English.

Letters, A Country Man. You have reported that in Australia's greeting to the Queen, to be given during the BBC's Round the World Christmas broadcast, a Mudgee boy, Ian Paterson, is to say: "I can talk beaut now."

The sentence is unfair to decent Australians and is in shocking bad taste.

Letters, Vera L Curtis. I am one "decent Aus-tralian" citizen who is not offended by the use of the word "beaut" in a little boy's tribute to the Queen.

1 would like to suggest that "A Country Man" should, before offering criticism of a script which was, doubtless, prepared by experts in their business of script writing, first remove the mote which is in his own eye. His statement that the word complained of is "in shocking bad taste" is more than shocking to me. In fact, it is a beaut exhibition of shockingly bad grammar.

Letters, G Williams. In preparation for the visit of the Queen, could we not tidy away such Americanisms as "bandwaggon" (the Prime Minister), "No dames for me!" (GPS schoolboy), "Take time off to," "Get tough with," "know-how," "buddy," etc.

A newspaper recently published a headline: "Queen holds down a big job!" Unpardonable.

Australian English, including slang, is Queen's English. Our unique and picturesque vocabulary should be preserved against intrusion.

OH NO! CHRISTMAS IS BACK AGAIN

It seems to happen every year, about this time. We always get one warm day (only) in early December, then about three weeks later, Christmas strikes. In the meantime, people seem to go off their rockers. They shop till they drop, they sit round in the open at night sniffing candle grease and chanting strange medieval songs, they buy things for each other that they would not think of buying at any other time, and they get in supplies of food to presumably keep them alive if they are besieged and isolated. On top of that, they go out and set records. A record number of people crowd the city, the crowds on the trains set records, the number of women fainting on Wynyard ramp is a record, the crowds of singers at Christmas carols are a record. It is a very strange period.

There were other alert people who had obviously noticed this odd herd-like behaviour in one way or another and, in 1953, were prepared to go into print.

Letters, Christopher. May I suggest that shops and stores place something in their decorations to remind us that Christmas is the birthday of Christ, the Saviour who was born in a manger?

By all means let us have a good time as only free people can; but let the significance of the day be remembered.

Comment. Record numbers of persons attended services this year, and doubtless prayed and sang at record levels. But outside of that, generally in the community and shops, references to Christianity's belief were well and truly down. This continued a trend since before 1950 that reversed the general swing to religion during the War years.

CHRISTMAS? NO PROBLEM

David Jones to the rescue. A special staff will work all through the night before Christmas Eve to fulfill Christmas orders at the Food Halls of David Jones Ltd. The December Food Fair is in full swing at both the Market Street and George Street stores, where a staff of over 300 food experts are ready to help the harassed housewife with her Christmas catering and eating-too-much problems.

Stocking the larder for the holiday season is usually a nightmare of shopping complicated by the extra provisioning needed to cope with unexpected visitors during the festive season. But at the DJ's Food Halls, in a matter of half an hour, and while keeping as cool as a cucumber in the air-conditioned atmosphere, the housewife can get her own special Christmas catering problem off her mind in advance – and on one spot. The rest is left to the specially trained staff of 300.

As most Christmas feasts centre around the poultry, it is consoling to know that every bird, whether turkey, chicken duck, or goose has been hand picked by DJ's food experts. For this reason it is advisable to order now. Buyers have estimated what is needed to supply customers' Christmas poultry needs and have bought accordingly.

If the estimate is exceeded they will have to disappoint rather than hurriedly buy what is left on the market at the last minute. This is DJ's own way of ensuring that all the poultry which goes out to the customers is of first class standard.

For those who fancy game there are large stocks of tinned partridge, pheasant, and grouse, imported from Scotland.

The not-to-be-forgotten Christmas ham is available in either the boned and canned Mayfair variety which ranges from the 2lb Mayfair baby to the 5½lb, 10 or 11lb family size, or mild-cured leg hams.

D J's model bakery has been busy for months turning out rich Christmas fruit cakes and puddings. The cakes and puddings are in "stock" sizes, ranging from 1lb to 6lb, but special weights can be made to order.

CHRISTMAS CHEER

Letters, V P. Last Saturday night a car was parked on the road outside my farm at Glenfield.

The road here is lined on my farm with beautiful 40-year-old pine trees, and with infinite care I had nursed for several years a few young ones to replace some which had died.

On Sunday morning I found that the nicest of the young trees, about 5 feet high, had been cut down and removed.

If this is the conception of the Christmas spirit, "Goodwill towards men," I am sorry.

Letters, Shopper. Couldn't we have quiet Christmas shopping this year?

Christmas carols and songs aren't meant to be played in department stores amid the rush and tear, when everyone's nerves are frayed, and when one is trying to think clearly what to buy for presents.

More than one salesgirl said to me last year – when carols were being played above the din – "I never thought I'd come to detest that tune!" I pity them, being there with it all day and every day.

These tunes are meant for the quiet and peace of Christmas.

SOME LITTLE THINGS FOR MEN

Normally, at this point in time, I abandon my Scrooge-like demeanour and talk about the goodies that people give as gifts. Women and children are normally covered quite well, but menfolk get little mention. This year, I have swung that round, and men take up all the available space.

Most of the major stores promote their sales for men by placing adverts that are persuasive rather than visual. Often reams of text are presented rather than a photo and a slogan.

A Case of Cawarra claret. Esquire feels that no meal is complete without "the living blood of the grape." Claret is a type-name applied to any dry, light table wine of ruby-red colour and contrary to popular opinion, is English; "clairette" is French, signifying a white wine. Cawarra bears the name of the oldest Australian vineyards in the Hunter Valley and produces a wine marked for its bouquet and balance. The Old Store will sell you a bottle delivered to your home for five shillings if you ring the Restaurant.

A Silver Match butane lighter. Science has finally come to the aid of the cigarette lighter, and not before time. Silver Match works on the usual principles – flint and a striking wheel, but it has no wick, only a steady stream of butane gas. This gives an unwavering, smokeless flame, that never misses. A three shilling refill cartridge holds approximately five thousand fires. You just flick the lighter and puff! A gentle, lambent flame. All for the picayune price of seventy shillings. The lighter is solid, sturdy and English. There are three designs, one plain and two fancy. The Ground Floor, Tobacco Department, please.

An English umbrella. The Royal Tour directors have laid down a dictum that umbrellas are preferable to rain-coats at official parties as they give a man a slightly martial appearance and walk. Down at the S for M they have some eight-rib English umbrellas that would have pleased Mr Chamberlain's and Anthony Eden's combined hearts. The shafts are steel, the frames Fox, the fabric silk, the ferrules steel, and the damage, eight pounds fifteen. Handles come in whangee or malacca cane. Furled, the umbrellas are as thin as a tooth-pick.

A pair of French braces. Esquire doesn't want to sound gossipy but something important is happening to the how-do-you-keep-your-pants-up problem. Braces are being seen on more and more backs around town – particularly narrower braces. Like the l'Aiglon braces on the Ground Floor. They are pigskin with elastic ends, rustless fittings, and satin linings. Two widths – three eighths of an inch for twenty-nine and six and one inch for thirty-two and six.

A pure silk Italian square. Florence, the Quattrocento, strange pleasures, strange people, the hills of flowery Tuscany – images invoked by Farmer's collection of Italian-patterned silks. Some have paisley, others figured medieval or architectural designs. All are sixty-two and six, with hand-rolled edges, in grey, green, blue and maroon. Rather than knot and crush them, use a hand-carved woggle, or wooden ring to catch the scarf at the neck. They're only four and six.

THE QUEEN'S ENGLISH.

I had thought that my coverage about the foibles of our pronunciation of the English language would just about put the subject to rest. But I was wrong. Letters on the subject kept turning up. Then, these four Letters below were printed on the Saturday before Christmas, so I knew they must be really important. Remember, they pertain to a lad who wanted to use the word "beaut" in an address to the Queen.

Letters, (Mrs) E Roussel. I am another decent Australian who is deeply shocked and even ashamed at the inclusion of the atrocious word "beaut" in any public tribute. Does the script writer concerned imagine that "current Australian" needs any further vulgarising? Consult any visitor.

Letters, J Brook. The sentence, "I can talk beaut now," is characteristic of the speech of many decent Australian boys. Does "A Country Man" wish to hear our youngsters attempt to ape a "Mayfair Accent" or speak in the style of an educated and mature adult?

This, apart from sounding unnatural, would be misleading and unfair to those listening to the broadcast.

Letters, J H Smith. Many Australians affect a careless and uneducated speech which has given the impression abroad that it is natural to all Australians. It would be unfortunate for this opinion officially to be endorsed in a world-wide broadcast.

The child will not be speaking informally, but will be giving a prepared speech on behalf of the nation.

Letters, Ronaldo. Everybody is making mountains out of dung hills. It is inevitable that a few bits of slang will creep into a language and that is what is happening.

It is not a case of a deluge of hundreds of new words being created, but instead just a few at a time are being improved.

There is nothing beautiful about a word. One word is just as beautiful as the next. What is important is what is conveyed by the word and the sentences that contain it.

If you want to improve the use of language, set laws that say that no persons can talk until they have thought about a matter for three seconds. And then set rules that say they cannot talk until they have thought about how much the listener already knows, and adjust their conversation accordingly.

Then we might get some decent communications.

SUMMING UP 1953

There is not much to say, really. The very good news was the end of the Korean War. The mind-numbing events were the Coronation, the coming Royal Visit, and the Melbourne Cup. But I know that most of you lap them up, so I will not even mention them. A few major crimes were shocking, the economy was fair enough, but could well be better. The lions in Coffs Harbour were very exciting, and the problems with stockings would continue for years.

What I am saying is that 1953 was a remarkably quiet year. **We were in fact blessed (again) by a shortage of terrible events, and there were no dreadful scares.** The world for Australians was all wrapped up in Australia, and we were left alone to go our own way. Maybe I am wrong, but I don't think you can ask for better than that. **If you were born in 1953, good luck, you are off to a flying start.**

COMMENTS FROM READERS

Tom Lynch, Speers Point…..Some history writers make the mistake of trying to boost their authority by including graphs and charts all over the place. You on the other hand get a much better effect by saying things like "he made a pile". Or "every one worked hours longer that they should have, and felt like death warmed up at the end of the shift." I have seen other writers waste two pages of statistics painting the same picture as you did in a few words….

Barry Marr, Adelaide….you know that I am being facetious when I say that I wish the War had gone on for years longer so that you would have written more books about it…

Edna College, Auburn…. A few times I stopped and sobbed as you brought memories of the postman delivering letters, and the dread that ordinary people felt as he neared. How you captured those feelings yet kept your coverage from becoming maudlin or bogged down is a wonder to me….

Betty Kelly. Every time you seem to be getting serious you throw in a phrase or memory that lightens up the mood. In particular, in the War when you were describing the terrible carnage of Russian troops, for no reason, you ended with a ten line description of how aggrieved you felt and ended it with "apart from that, things are pretty good here". For me, it turned the unbearable into the bearable, and I went from feeling morbid and angry back to a normal human being….

Alan Davey, Brisbane….I particularly liked the light-hearted way you described the scenes at the airports as the American high-flying entertainers flew in. I had always seen the crowd behaviour as disgraceful, but your light-hearted description of it made me realise it was in fact harmless and just good fun….

In 1954, Queen Elizabeth II was sent here victorious, and Petrov was our very own spy - what a thrill. Boys were being sentenced to life. Johnny Ray cried all the way to the bank. Church halls were being used for dirty dancing. Open the pubs after six? Were they ever shut? A-bombs had scaredies scared.

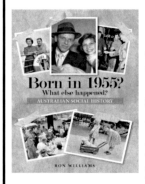

In 1955, be careful of the demon drink, get your brand new Salk injections, submit your design for the Sydney Opera house now, prime your gelignite for another Redex Trial, and stop your greyhounds killing cats. Princess Margaret shocked the Church, Huxley shocked the Bishops, and our Sundays are far from shocking.

****

There are 35 books in this Series. One each year from 1939 to 1973.

In 1956, the first big issue was the Suez crisis, which put our own Bob Menzies on the world stage, but he got no applause. TV was turned on in time for the Melbourne Olympics, Hungary was invaded and the Iron Curtain got a lot thicker. There was much concern about cruelty to sharks, and the horrors of country pubs persisted.

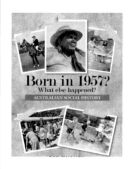

In 1957, Britain's Red Dean said Chinese Reds were OK. America avoided balance-of-payments problems by sending entertainers here. Sydney's Opera House will use lotteries to raise funds. The Russians launched Sputnik and a dog got a free ride. A bodkin crisis shook the nation.

****

Chrissi and birthday books for Mum and Dad and Aunt and Uncle and cousins and family and friends and work and everyone else.

Don't forget a good read and chuckle for yourself.

Born in 1958?
What else happened?
AUSTRALIAN SOCIAL HISTORY

RON WILLIAMS

In 1958, the Christian brothers bought a pub and raffled it; some clergy thought that Christ would not be pleased. Circuses were In 1956, the first big issue was the Suez crisis, which put our own Bob Menzies on the world stage, but he got no applause. TV was turned on in time for the Melbourne Olympics, Hungary was invaded and the Iron Curtain got a lot thicker. There was much concern about cruelty to sharks, and the horrors of country pubs persisted.

****

AVAILABLE AT ALL GOOD BOOK STORES AND NEWSAGENTS